AWESOME POWER FROM ON HIGH
—Praise—

I have known Brother Bob Canton for many years in his healing ministry. In all of my observations of him, he is a humble man filled with the Holy Spirit. He allows the Glory of God to pass through him as a healing instrument of Jesus. Brother Bob's gift of healing reminds me of the Gospel story in John, chapter five, about the man who was sick for thirty-eight years, waiting to go into the pool called Bethesda, a place where the blind, lame, and crippled could go to be healed. When Jesus encountered this man, He asked him if he wanted to be made well. The sick man replied and explained that he had no one to put him into the pool. Jesus simply told him to rise and take up his mat and walk. Immediately, the man became well.

I share this story because it reminds me of Bob Canton, as he also speaks healing to the sick, and they are healed by the power of Jesus. Brother Bob Canton allows the Holy Spirit to guide him through his many healing services all over the world. His faith is strong. He trusts that God is using him to heal His people. He gives our Lord all the glory for the many healings that take place. Bob Canton is also a good teacher because he studies the scriptures and presents these as inspiring lessons during his healing services. The scriptures are in his heart. He is a man filled with the Spirit of God.

PRAISE

If you ever have the opportunity to see Brother Bob if he is in your town, go and witness God at work through this wonderful man. I feel honored and privileged to know him.

—Sally Ann Quiñones—

Author, *Everlasting Grace*

Awesome Power from on High by Bob Canton is the most systematic and detailed presentation on the Holy Spirit and His gifts I have seen in the recent times. It gives excellent teachings on the gifts based on scripture references, quotes from the Fathers of the Church, and testimonies from Bob's own ministry powered by the charisms given by the Holy Spirit.

Bob was an active member of the International Catholic Charismatic Renewal Services (ICCRS) Council and has travelled to all parts of the world for ministry.

There have been many testimonies of healing during his ministry. He has a track record of an exemplary life of submission to authorities, love for the Church, commitment to the call, and using the charisms for building up the Body of Christ.

The book is a timely blessing to the Church and the Renewal. I feel that we need to have such deeper understanding of the power of the Holy Spirit, and we need to receive the charisms and put them to use for building up the Church, especially during this turbulent time. I know for certain that the readers of this book cannot remain the same. They are going to be impacted greatly through the teachings and testimonies.

PRAISE

May this book help in ushering in a new Pentecost in the Church that we have been praying for faithfully.

—Cyril John—
Member of CHARIS & Chairman,
ICCRS Sub-Committee for Asia-Oceania (ISAO)

In this much needed and updated presentation on the Gifts of the Holy Spirit, Bob invites us to see these gifts as necessary tools for the New Evangelization.

God's awesome power is explained through the use of scripture, personal experience, and expectant faith that these gifts should be normative in the life of every baptized Christian.

—Deacon Larry and Andi Oney—
Hope and Purpose Ministries

Bob Canton has again provided us with an inspiring and challenging book, *Awesome Power from On High,* that weaves scripture, Church teaching, and personal experience and reflection. Quite frankly, I could not put it down. I felt convicted when he challenges the reader to be more open to the awesome power of God: not only to believe in it, but also more importantly to act upon it. There is never, however, a note of condemnation, rather always encouragement.

I heartily recommend this book to all who want to grow in their expectant faith and in their acting in trust to bring healing of all kinds in the name of Jesus, our Lord.

—Walter Matthews—
Executive Director
National Service Committee
of the Catholic Charismatic Renewal, U.S.

AWESOME POWER FROM ON HIGH

AWESOME POWER FROM ON HIGH

"Learn how to receive the awesome power of God and how to use it in your everyday life."

Stockton, CA
Robert "Bob" Canton

*To my late parents
Lily and Petronilo Canton,
and to my wife Chita,
my two daughters
Stephanie and Tricia,
my grandchildren
Jordyn Grace Marie and
Logan Anthony,
my son-in-law Jason Galvez,
and to my entire family and friends who give
their full and unwavering support
and offer their prayers to the Lord
for my works in His vineyard,
I dedicate this book.*

—Contents—

—Preface—

Praise the Name of Jesus, now and forever!

After my first book, *"Miracles Never Ending,"* was out, I received nothing but great reports from people who had read it. Many of them have even sent me testimonies of healings and restorations after they had been praying the specific prayers for specific illnesses contained in the book plus the "Healing and Keeping Prayer," "Prayer for Empowerment," and "Spiritual Warfare Prayer."

Some of my friends had asked me if I plan to write another book. I told them that if the Holy Spirit would prompt me and inspire me to write another book, I certainly would do it. If the Lord wills it, it will certainly happen, no doubt.

Last September 2018, while on route to Toronto, Canada, from Halifax, Nova Scotia, after speaking and ministering during the Catholic Charismatic Convention, I asked the Lord to give me a sign that He wants me to write another book. The Lord spoke into my heart. He said, "My son, I want you to write a book on the Gifts of my Holy Spirit. I want my children to be more equipped to do the works that I want them to do through the power of my Holy Spirit to further my Father's Kingdom. Rely on me; rely on the power of my Holy Spirit, not only sometimes nor oftentimes, but all of the time. I love you my son."

I found out, especially during the time of ministering to the people of God, that many are not conversant, familiar, nor even aware of the nine 'Charismatic' gifts of the Holy Spirit as enumerated by St. Paul in 1Corinthians, chapter twelve. These gifts are word of wisdom, word of knowledge, faith, healing, miracles, prophecy, tongues, interpretation of tongues, and discernment of spirits. They are given by the Holy Spirit to serve and to build up the Church and His people for the glory of God. These gifts are also called the "Charismatic gifts," taken from a Greek word, 'Charismata,' or favor freely given by God to whomever He chooses.

In obedience to and in compliance with the Lord's instructions and desires, this book, *Awesome Power from On High*, is about the *nine* gifts of the Holy Spirit.

However, many are more familiar with the seven gifts of the Holy Spirit, namely: wisdom, understanding, counsel, fortitude, knowledge, piety, and fear of God. We can read about these gifts in Isaiah, chapter eleven. Another description for these kinds of gifts is 'Isaiah'n gifts.' These are given by God for personal sanctification. These gifts, according to St. Thomas of Aquinas, are *habits, instincts,* or *dispositions* provided by God as supernatural helps to man in the process of his *perfection*. They enable man to transcend the limitations of human reason and human nature and participate in the very life of God, as Christ promised. St. Thomas of Aquinas insisted that they are necessary for man's salvation, which he cannot achieve on his own.

In mid January 2019, I started writing the manuscript. Although I didn't have a chance to work on this book daily because of my busy ministry schedule plus having to spend quality time with my family, I was able to finish writing this book towards the end of March 2019.

No doubt, the Holy Spirit has helped me more than I could have possibly imagined. After all, He is our Helper! Glory be to God! I was amazed at how He reminded me and guided me to relate many events that took place in my life that are relevant and significant to the subject matter I'm talking about. He also sufficiently furnished me with passages from the scriptures, the teachings contained in the *Catechisms of the Catholic Church,* and from the writings of the Fathers of the Catholic Church that provide emphasis, support, and credibility to the teachings of the different gifts of the Holy Spirit.

Therefore, I would like to thank the Holy Spirit, first of all, for His inspiration, guidance, and wisdom in making this book, *Awesome Power from On High,* a reality.

The works of the Holy Spirit in the mighty Name of Jesus are indeed awesome for the glory of God the Father.

Praise and glory to the Holy Trinity, forever and ever!

I would also like to express my heartfelt thanks to my friends, Walter Matthews, Executive Director of the Catholic Charismatic Renewal in the U.S., Deacon Larry and his wife Andi Oney, Cyril John, Sally Ann Quiñones, all authors in their own rights who wrote endorsements for this book, and Bonnie Crutcher, who did all the work such as consulting, copyediting, typesetting, designing, coordinating the printing, and all the preparations to make this book ready for printing and publication.

Last but not least, I would like to thank my family members including my wife and two daughters, my son-in-law, my two grandchildren, my late parents, all my family members and friends, specially all the members of the Children of God Prayer Community of St. Luke's Parish, Stockton, all the officers and coordinators and spiritual advisers of the Alliance of Filipino Catholic Charismatic Prayer Communities in North America (AFCCPC), the president, vice-president, the director and council members of the Vatican-based International Catholic Charismatic Renewal Services (ICCRS), all those who sent me their testimonies of healings and miracles and restorations for the glory of God, as well as countless people from many parts of the world who have been praying daily for me, my family, and for my ministry. To all of you, I would like to express my deepest gratitude.

In closing, please allow me to encourage you to always put these words according to Philippians 4:19 into your heart, "But my God shall supply all your need according to his riches in glory by Christ Jesus."

To God be the glory, forever and ever, Amen!

CHAPTER 1
The Awesome Power
of the
Holy Spirit

In John 14:16-17, Jesus says:

> *And I will ask the Father and he*
> *will give you another Advocate,*
> *to be with you always, the Spirit*
> *of truth, which the world cannot*
> *accept, because it neither sees*
> *nor knows him. But you know*
> *him, because he remains with*
> *you, and will be in you.*

The English word advocate is the source word for para-clete. It is derived from Latin words "ad," meaning "to," and "vocata," meaning "somebody called to **or** in."

The word advocate is discriptive for a lawyer. It means someone who speaks in our defense or on our behalf. The word "paraclete" is taken from the Latin word, "paracletus," meaning "a person who is called in along-side to assist or help," or someone who can do something for you that you cannot do for yourself.

While ministering in Malaysia not too long ago, I wit-nessed many people, mostly women, who were oppressed by evil spirits. Some were crawling on the floor like snakes and barking like dogs while others were shouting at the top of their voices and spewing venomous, unprintable words. All of a sudden, a man stood up from the floor with both hands extended towards me, aiming for my neck. His eyes and demeanor were full of wrath, and he kept on saying, "I'm going to kill you, I'm going to kill you." Some people had run away, obviously in great fright. For a split second, the Lord spoke into my heart. He said, "My son, fear not. I'm here with you; my angels are with you. I want you to rebuke the spirits of violence and anger and divination and murder, in my Name." I did what the Lord had instructed me to do.

Seconds later, when the man was only a few feet away from me, he stopped dead in his tracks, unable to move. Afterwards, he fell down to the floor. I was able to say a deliverance prayer over him, in Jesus' mighty name, and then he calmed down. He told me that he felt like his body was shackled with steel and his feet were glued to the floor. He said he tried with all of his strength to move, but to no avail. He could not move and was unable to lift up neither his hands nor his feet, until he fell down.

I told this man that the power of the evil one is no match, not even close, to the power of the Holy Spirit—Alleluia!

When I talked to this man afterwards, I found out that he had many mistresses, he had used services of prostitutes, he had been stoned with drugs, he had been an alcoholic, and he had also dabbled in the occult: tarot cards, Quija boards, seances, and divination. I told him that he was an easy prey of the evil one. I then encouraged him to go to confession that very day, attend Mass daily for at least thirty days without interruption, pray the Rosary daily, pray before the Blessed Sacrament daily, say the Litany of the Precious Blood daily and, most of all, to lead a clean and Holy life. I then led him to renounce the evil practices that he had been doing, in the name and by the precious blood of Jesus. I told this man that he had to close the door that he had opened wide to the evil one by what he had been doing.

In John 10:10, Jesus says: "Satan comes only to kill, to slaughter and to destroy. I have come to give you life, a life in abundance."

Two years prior, a similar scenario took place in the big hall in the Blessed Sacrament Parish in Kuching, Sarawak, Malaysia. A person named Valentine Lim also tried to attack me in the church during the Healing Crusade.

I believe when the Holy Spirit is present, the evil spirits cannot stand His presence and His anointing. (Kindly see the chapter on the Spiritual Gift of Discernment of Spirits for more insight.)

Who is the Holy Spirit?

The Holy Spirit is God. He is the Third Person of the Trinity, co-equal and co-substantial with God the Father and God the Son. He is not a a ghost or a concept. He is not a white cloud. He is not a dove. He is a person possessing a will, an intellect, and emotions.

The Holy Spirit is called the Advocate, the Comforter, the Counselor, an Intercessor, a Helper, a Standby, a Strengthener, a Teacher, a Guide, a Love between the Father and the Son, and the Uncreated Power of God.

The Catechism of the Catholic Church #693 states:

> Besides the proper name of 'Holy Spirit,' which is most frequently used in the *Acts of the*

Apostles and in the Epistles, we also find in St. Paul the titles: the Spirit of the promise,[1] the Spirit of adoption,[2] the Spirit of Christ,[3] the Spirit of the Lord,[4] and the Spirit of God[5]—and, according to St. Peter, the Spirit of glory.[6]

The Roles of the Holy Spirit in a Person's Life

The roles of the Holy Spirit are indeed varied and numerous. Allow me to cite at least a few.

A. Jesus says that the Holy Spirit is our Advocate, our Paraclete, our Comforter.

We don't need anyone or anything more than the Holy Spirit. Many people, sad to say, have very little idea of the reality of what the Holy Spirit came to do in us on a continual basis.

In John 16:7, Jesus says: But I tell you the truth, it is better for you that I go. For if I do not go, the Advocate will not come to you.…

One of the biggest reasons, based on the words of Jesus, as to why He died on the Cross at Calvary, is for the Holy Spirit to live and dwell within us. In John 7:37, Jesus exclaimed:

> …Let anyone who thirsts come to me and drink. Whoever believes in me, as scripture says:
>
> "Rivers of living water will flow from within him."

The Holy Spirit dwells in us. We are His temple. The Word of God says in 1 Corinthians 3:16: "Do you not know that you are the temple of God, and that the Spirit of God dwells in you?"

The Holy Spirit is our Helper. He is here to guide us, strengthen us, and equip us. When we are in the midst of a storm in our life, we need to call on the Holy Spirit to help us. We can always depend on Him. We do not need to rely only on our friends and relatives or on our own wisdom and knowledge, or strength or power. Instead, we can rely on the Comforter, the Holy Spirit who guides us and leads us to the right path and in the right direction for the fullness of life and on to victory.

B. The Holy Spirit glorifies Jesus and leads us into all truths.

In the Upper Room, on the eve of His crucifixion, Jesus said to his disciples:

> The Advocate, the holy Spirit that the Father will send in my name—he will teach you everything and remind you of all that [I]told you. (John 14:26)

In John 16:14, Jesus says: "He will glorify me because he will take from what is mine and declare it to you."

The Holy Spirit will make Jesus and the things of God real to you and me. He enables us to know Jesus and gives us the power to live and do His works and share the abundant life to all who obey and trust Him. He will make the Word of God alive in our hearts as we read the scriptures.

It is the Holy Spirit who makes the Word of God relevant and meaningful in our lives. He inspired holy and Godly men of old to write His words.

Jesus said in John 6:63: "…The words I have spoken to you are spirit and life."

We cannot live a holy and blessed life apart from the power of the Holy Spirit. Without the help and the power of the Holy Spirit, it is impossible for us to have a vibrant prayer life, to understand the Bible and other spiritual truths, to witness or do anything for the Lord, to become the person the Lord wants us to be, and to live a victorious life.

In Ephesians 5:18, St. Paul says: "And do not get drunk on wine, in which lies debauchery, but be filled with the Spirit,…"

To be filled with the Spirit is to be filled with Jesus, who is the baptizer of the Holy Spirit.

As Christians, we should strive to become more like Jesus in every way. The only way we can become more like Jesus is through the help of the Holy Spirit and bearing the fruits of love, joy, peace, patience, kindness, gentleness, generosity, faithfulness, and self-control (see Galatians 5:22-23). Without possessing the Holy Spirit, it is impossible for anyone to bear such fruit and be like Jesus.

C. The Holy Spirit equips and empowers believers.

In Acts 1:8, Jesus says:

> But you will receive power when the holy Spirit comes upon you, and you will be my witnesses in Jerusalem, throughout Judea and Samaria, and to the ends of the earth.

As baptized believers, we are imbued with power from on high. We have received the same power that raised Jesus from the dead.

On one occasion during my ministry I had the privilege to conduct a Growth in the Spirit seminar in St. Christopher Church in Ontario, California. Before taking our lunch break, I requested the members of the music ministry to sing some praise and worship songs. The songs were powerful and Spirit-filled and they touched the hearts of the attendees. Then, all of a sudden, I heard the voice of the Lord saying into my heart, "My son, breathe on them." I thought the Lord's instruction was for me to go to each person individually and literally "breathe on them."

The Lord spoke again into my heart, "My son, I want you to use the microphone to breathe on my people. Know my son, it's not your "breath" but the breath of my Holy Spirit."

As soon as I obeyed the Lord by releasing a resounding "breath" into the microphone, every one of the more than one hundred fifty people present fell down on the floor like an accordion, together with their chairs. Many of them instantly received the gift of tongues, and others prophesied.

After about fifteen minutes or so had elapsed, they all stood up and ran towards me. My three companions from Stockton were so scared that they joined their extended hands around me to "protect" me. I told my friends not to worry, because the attendees just wanted me to pray over them. Many also received physical, mental, emotional, and no doubt, spiritual healing from the Lord Jesus.

For sure the people were in awe of the manifestations of the power of the Holy Spirit. Even though they fell down on the floor together with their chairs, they told me that they were not hurt nor injured whatsoever.

The same manifestation of God's power occurred eight months later in St. Clement's Church in Stamford, Connecticut. It was indeed one of the most awesome powers that I have ever witnessed so far.

The power of the Holy Spirit is manifested through the gifts of the Holy Spirit.

In 1 Corinthians 12:4–11, St. Paul explains:

> There are different kinds of spiritual gifts but the same Spirit; there are different forms of service but the same Lord; there are different workings but the same God who produces all of them in everyone. To each individual the manifestation of the Spirit is given for some benefit. To one is given through the Spirit the expression of wisdom; to another the expression of knowledge according to the same Spirit; to another faith by the same Spirit; to another gifts of healing by the one Spirit; to another mighty deeds; to another prophecy; to another discernment of spirits; to another varieties of tongues; to another interpretation of tongues. But one and the same Spirit produces all of these, distributing them individually to each person as he wishes.

These gifts of the Holy Spirit are designed to serve and to build up the Body of Christ.

What is the Pauline Teaching on the Roles of the Holy Spirit in a Person's Life?

St. Paul teaches that the roles of the Holy Spirit in a person's life are as follows:

- He is the Spirit of Power (1 Corinthians 2–4; Romans 15:13; 1 Thessalonians 1:5).
- He reveals God's wisdom to men (1 Corinthians 2:10; John 14:26).
- He helps us to pray (Romans 8:26).
- He frees us from the law and the bondage of the flesh (Romans 8:2–11).

We need the Person and the gifts of the Holy Spirit to do the works of Jesus. The spiritual gifts are God's manifestation of His presence and power in and through individuals and groups of believers. It is indeed very exciting to be alive in this day and age because the Holy Spirit is still very active in the world today. These *grace moments,* the powerful manifestations of God's presence and power, are indeed still available to any believer who is a yielded vessel to His Spirit. Therefore, to receive and experience these "grace moments" from the Lord, all we have to do is open our hearts wide to our Lord Jesus Christ and say, with faith and expectation, "Come Lord Jesus, and fill me with your Holy Spirit and with your power."

WCR This Week
"Outpouring of Spirit's healing highlights lay evangelist's service"
June 1, 2015
THANDIWE KONGUAVI
WESTERN CATHOLIC REPORTER

EDMONTON—When Robert Canton woke up on Pentecost Day this year, he was excited. In Edmonton from his home in Stockton, Calif., for the New Evangelization and Healing Conference, invited for his talent of the charismatic gift of healing, he knew the Lord was going to do something big. After all, it was the day of Pentecost, the "birthday" of the Church, when the Holy Spirit descended upon Jesus' disciples. Already during the three-day conference at Edmonton's Mary Help of Christians Chinese Catholic Church, testimonies of miraculous healing through the Holy Spirit had been pouring in. "The Holy Spirit is very alive and still active nowadays," said the lay evangelist. "That's why I'm very excited." So Canton asked the Holy Spirit what he should say to the 300 or so expectant people who came to the third day of the conference on Sunday. "I want them to know more of my Holy Spirit, because many of them don't have any idea what the Holy Spirit can do for them and through them," Canton said the Lord spoke into his heart. Then, following his talk, he did a demonstration.

Many people lined up in faith hoping for the healing of infirmities such as cancer, deafness and lameness. They were not disappointed. Canes, walkers and glasses were discarded and $6,000 hearing aids thrown aside, as many people heard clearly for the first time in years, saw clearly for the first time in years and walked boldly for the first time in years drawing tears from astonished audience members.

MANY HEALINGS

Cancer healing testimonies from the event have yet to be confirmed, but previous miracles performed through Canton, a member of the Vatican-based International Catholic Charismatic Renewal Services, include healing from cancer and infertility, and raising the dead back to life." We should all be making the blind see," he said. When Jesus raised the dead to life, healed the blind and the deaf, and proclaimed the Gospel, he did it all by the power of the Holy Spirit." If Jesus had to rely on the power of the Holy Spirit, how much more that we should rely on the power of the Holy Spirit," he said. Cory Yakimovich, chair of Catholic Renewal Services of Edmonton, said "Many people were very grateful that [Canton] came, very blessed that he came. They hadn't seen the Lord work in signs and wonders like this before."

Source: Permission given by the Western Catholic Reporter–c/0 Corrine Yarmakovich, Chair, Catholic Charismatic Renewal Board, Edmonton, Alberta, Canada.

Part of the audience during the Southern Catholic Charismatic Conference in Metaire, Louisiana, a suburb of New Orleans, in September 2018. Robert was speaker in the conference.

Chapter 1 Endnotes

1. Cf. Gal 3:14; Eph 1:13.
2. Rom 8:15; Gal 4:6.
3. Rom 8:9.
4. 2 Cor 3:17.
5. Rom 8:9, 14; 15:19; 1 Cor 6:11; 7:40.
6. 1 Pet 4:14.

CHAPTER 2
Overview
of the Gifts
of the Holy Spirit

Now in regard to spiritual gifts,
brothers, I do not want you to be
unaware.

In 1 Corinthians 12:8–10, St. Paul describes the following charismatic gifts: the word of wisdom, the word of knowledge, faith, healing, miracles, prophecy, discernment of spirits, tongues, and interpretation of tongues. These gifts are the ingredients for a powerful and effective work of evangelization.

The Catechism of the Catholic Church, #798, states:

> ...by the many special graces (called "charisms"), by which he makes the faithful "fit and ready to undertake various tasks and offices for the renewal and building up of the Church."[1]

The charisms are not just natural abilities rather gifts given by the Holy Spirit to each person as He wills.

Other gifts are mentioned in Ephesians 4, Romans 12, and 1 Peter 4. Surely the charisms, or spiritual gifts, manifest the transcendence of God.

I had the honor and the privilege not too long ago to conduct Healing Crusades in Thailand and Malaysia, in Denmark, Finland, Norway, Sweden, Japan, Singapore, Hong Kong, and in many other parts of the world. During those crusades, the manifestations of the gifts of the Holy Spirit such as the word of knowledge, prophecy, healings, miracles, tongues, word of wisdom, and tongues with interpretation of tongues were very visible and prominent. Some people walked from wheelchairs, deaf people were able to hear, tumors and abnormal growths disappeared, some blind people regained their sight, and other healings such as emotional, spiritual, mental, and healings involving relationships as well as deliverance from evil spirits took place.

Afterwards, some non-Christians came up to us asking to be baptized as Roman Catholics because they had witnessed the power and presence of Jesus in their midst. They came to believe in the preaching that Jesus is true God and true man who died for our sins, who rose from the dead, and who is now seated at the right hand of God interceding for us all.

These new believers came to believe that Jesus is the Divine Healer, and that He is still healing by the power of the Holy Spirit.

Jesus said in John 14:11:

> Believe me that I am in the Father and the
> Father is in me, or else, believe because of the
> works themselves.

The Early Church Fathers were ancient writers and Christian theologians. These men are called the Fathers of the Church because of their leadership in the early

Church in expounding, developing, and defending the Catholic doctrines.

Now, let us read what some of the Fathers of the Church said about the Spiritual Gifts.

IRENAEUS
The Overseer of the Church
at Lyons in France
A.D. 115? 125? to 202

In his writings Irenaeus defends the gifts of the Holy Spirit. He writes in book 2:

> Even among the brethren frequently in a case of necessity, when the whole church united in much fasting and prayer, the spirit has returned to the ex-animated body, and the man was granted to the prayers of the saints.

After some other observations he writes:

> But if they say that our Lord also did these things only in appearance, we shall refer them back to the prophetic declarations, and shall show from them that all these things were strictly foretold, and were done by Him and that He alone is the Son of God. Wherefore, also, those who were truly His disciples, receiving grace from Him, in His name per-

formed these things for the benefit of the rest of men, as everyone received the free gift from Him. Some, indeed, most certainly and truly cast out demons, so that frequently those persons themselves were cleansed from wicked spirits, believed and were received into the Church. Others have the knowledge of things to come, as also visions and prophetic communications; others heal the sick by the imposition of hands, and restore them to health. And, moreover, as we said above, even the dead have been raised, and continued with us for many years. And why should we say more? It is impossible to tell the number of gifts which the Church throughout the world received from God, and the deeds performed in the name of Jesus Christ that was crucified under Pontius Pilate, and this to every day for the benefit of the heathen, without deceiving any, or exacting their money. For as she has received freely from God, she also ministers. Nor does she perform anything by means of angelic invocations or by incantations, or by any other wicked, curious art; but directing her prayers to the Lord who made all things, in a pure, sincere and straightforward spirit, and calling upon the name of our Lord Jesus Christ, she has been accustomed to work miracles for the advantage of mankind, and not to lead them into error.

The name of our Lord Jesus Christ EVEN NOW confers benefits, and cures thoroughly and effectually ALL who ANYWHERE believe on Him.

In book 5 Irenaeus writes:

> In like manner do we also hear many brethren in the Church who possess prophetic gifts, who through the Spirit speak all kinds of languages, and bring to light for the general benefit the hidden things of men and declare the mysteries of God, whom also the apostles term spiritual gifts.

ORIGEN
A.D. 185 to 254

In defending Christianity from the attacks of Celsus, an arch opponent of Christianity, Origen tells how he had seen with his own eyes the healing of grievous diseases and the insane by invocation of the name of God and Jesus. He states in "Against Celsus" 3.24:

> And some give evidence of having received, through their faith, a marvellous power, by the cures which they perform, invoking no other name over those who need their help than that of the God of all things, and of Jesus, along with mention of his history. For we too HAVE SEEN many persons freed by these means, from grievous calamities and from distractions of mind and from madness and from countless other ills which could not be cured either by men or devils.

AUGUSTINE
A.D. 354 to 430

In about A.D. 390, Augustine wrote the following in his treatise, "On the True Religion":

> For when the Catholic Church had been diffused and established through the whole world, those miracles were no longer permitted to continue in our time, lest the mind should always seek visible things, and the human race should be chilled by the customariness of the very things whose novelty had inflamed them.

This was written about four or five years after Augustine's conversion, and it could be that the young convert accepted and quoted the views of some of the spiritual leaders around him. However, shortly before his death in A.D. 430, Augustine admitted that he had not told the truth, and in His work, "Retractions" 1.13.7., he retracted what he had written in, "On the True Religion," and stated that even when he wrote it, he had known of a blind man being healed in Milan, and other miracles. What integrity! It was a good thing that he repented and decided to tell the truth. Some thirty-seven years after writing, "On the True Religion," Augustine wrote at length, in about A.D. 427, about miracles taking place in his day; he states in "The City of God," book 22, chapter 8: "Even now miracles are wrought in the name of Christ."

These spiritual gifts are not only applicable during Healing Crusades or Healing Services or Healing Rallies or prayer meetings, but they can also be used in the marketplace, in the workplace, at home or wherever there are human interactions.

The Vatican Council 2 document on the Decree of the Apostolate of Lay People, Section 3, asserts:

> From the reception of these charisms, even the most ordinary ones, there arises each of the faithful the right and the duty of exercising them in the Church and in the world for the good of men and development of the Church, of exercising the freedom of the Holy Spirit who 'breathes where He wills.'

I vividly remember a time when Emmanuel, a member of our Children of God Prayer Community music ministry group of St. Luke's Parish in Stockton, California, and I were about to fly out of Sacramento International Airport going to Las Vegas, Nevada, to conduct a workshop on healing and to hold a Healing Rally.

On the airplane before we took off, a vacant seat was between us. However, ten minutes before the airplane took off, a young man in his mid-twenties and smiling from ear to ear occupied that seat between Emmanuel and me. He was obviously very excited to be on that flight. He introduced himself to us, and Emmanuel and I introduced ourselves to him. He said, "Oh, man, I can hardly wait to be in Las Vegas!"

"Mark, you seem very excited. What are you going to do in Vegas?", I inquired of him. He said, "Tonight, I'm going to attend a Bachelor's party. Man, it's gonna be wild," he informed us. So, I asked him how wild would it be. He whispered into my ears. I responded, "Yes, I cannot believe how wild it's going to be."

Mark told me things that he and his friends were going to do, things that I would not dare print in this book. And he reminded us, "What happens in Vegas, stays in Vegas, you know."

Mark then turned to me and asked, "How about the two of you? What are you going to do in Vegas?" I thought to myself, *Alleluia! I believe he knows how to ask the right questions.*

I then told Mark that we were going to preach the Word of God and conduct a Healing Rally in Jesus' Name. I told him that when I was younger and single and "foolish," I did some "wild" things also, maybe "more wild" than what he is doing now.

I told him that one time I took a bullet train doing 350 miles per hour from downtown Paris, France, to Notre Dame Du Laus. I explained in comparison how I had once been going to hell faster than a bullet train in France. However, the Lord in His mercy and His undying love and compassion for me and for all of us, had saved me from the clutches of the enemy of our souls. I explained how I asked Him to come into my life and be the Lord and Savior of my life. As a result, I have peace and joy and excitement and exhilaration in my heart knowing that the Lord is walking with me and loving me and using me and protecting me and providing and caring for me in spite of myself. I could hardly wait to wake up in the morning because I know that the Lord has new revelations for me every day.

I told Mark also what St. Augustine says, "My heart is restless, O Lord, until it rests in you." "You see Mark," I further stated, "there is a Jesus-sized space in our heart that only He can fill. If Jesus is not in that space, we seek and seek, and then sometimes we seek in the wrong places. That's why most of the time, we have somebody else or something else in that spot. Many, sad to say, indulged in worldly things such as alcohol, drugs, sex, money, gambling, and other vices. As a result, we feel frustrated and disillusioned and hopeless, and we become depressed and defeated. We need to seek Jesus in our heart, really seek Him and follow Him and walk with Him every day. Otherwise, we become like a zombie, a dead man walking, and we become like a corpse, spiritually, mentally and emotionally."

I quoted to Mark what St. Paul says in Romans 6:23: "For the wages of sin is death, but the gift of God is eternal life in Christ Jesus our Lord." Emmanuel also shared his testimony with Mark on how the Lord has touched his heart and his life, and as a result, he has become a new person inside.

Mark told us that his brother who lives in Colorado is a Christian and that he goes to church on a regular basis. I told Mark that I would not be surprised that his brother has been praying for him. "Maybe his prayer is like this: 'Please Lord, put Mark in between two Christians who are willing to talk to him about you,'" I told him in a half-joking kind of way.

Then I told Mark that the Lord has a reason why He opened doors for the three of us to be seated next to one another. I then asked him if he was willing to pray with us. At first, he was kind of hesitant, and checked if somebody was watching us, but then he said, "Okay." I immediately grabbed his right hand, and Emmanuel took Mark's left hand. We prayed together, asking the Holy Spirit to touch Mark's life in Jesus' Name. I led him to say the "Forgiveness" prayer, and a prayer to invite Jesus to be the Lord and Savior of his life.

The flight took one and one-half hours, but it seemed like it took only thirty minutes. We said our good-byes when we arrived at the airport in Las Vegas, and I reminded Mark not to forget that God truly loves him.

Emmanuel and I then took the shuttle at the airport and headed to the baggage claim area. While waiting for our luggage, I felt a tap on my back. When I looked back, it was Mark. He said to me, "Bob, man, I will never forget you, man." He said this with tears in his eyes. I told him without hesitation whatsoever, "Mark if you forget me, you don't lose anything. But if you forget the Lord, you will lose everything." It must have been the Holy Spirit who prompted me to say these words to him. Mark just turned around and left, while wiping away his tears.

Emmanuel and I made some conjecture or maybe a wild speculation that Mark had taken the next flight out headed back to Sacramento. Maybe it was just a "wishful thinking" on our part; only God knows, of course. However, we had the opportunity to minister to him through the promptings of the Holy Spirit.

I firmly believe that what happened to Mark on the airplane on the way to Las Vegas should not "stay in Vegas," but should be proclaimed throughout the world that the Lord wants to break through our broken world to reach out to us in order to make us whole and to set us free from the hands of the enemy. Sometimes, He uses very ordinary people just like you and me to reach out to the brokenhearted, to the suffering, and to the downtrodden to assure them that He loves them and He cares for them more than they could possibly imagine. Blessed be the name of the Lord!

I would like to state here, that through the nudging and leadings and promptings of the Holy Spirit, I have had many occasions when the Lord allowed me to minister to people. He has led me to minister in airports, airplanes, banks, marketplaces, restaurants, hotels, hospitals, and one time, in a Women's Prison, as well as many other places where He had put me to be the vessel of His ever-flowing power and love. I cannot thank Him enough for equipping me with His gifts to do His works.

Not too long ago, I was in Dubai, UAE to conduct Healing Crusades in this Arab country. I was scheduled to conduct a three-day Healing Crusade in St. Mary's Church, the largest Catholic parish in the world.

It has close to 400,000 parishioners with Masses offered in more than twelve languages every Sunday.

A priest in that parish talked to me and asked me if I could go with him and the leader of the music ministry to a bar/house of prostitution to invite the women to attend the Healing Crusade. The priest told me that it would be better if I could go with them so that I could invite the prostitutes personally, since I would be the one to conduct the Healing Crusade. At first, I was very hesitant to go with them. He said there are women from different countries including Filipino women, Russians, Malaysians, Chinese, Indonesians, Lithuanians, and other women from European and African countries. The priest had further informed me that many of them were Christian women, and many were Roman Catholics, but many of them were no longer practicing their faith for obvious reasons. "Even if only one person would come, there is a big potential that the Holy Spirit could touch that person's life," the priest tried to convince me. Because of his insistence for me to go with them, I acceded to do it.

Needless to say, I was a little bit nervous when we were inside the bar of the house of prostitution. I asked the Lord to cover all of us inside the building with His most precious blood and to protect all of us from the forces of darkness. The priest did not wear his priestly garb. He then invited ten women to sit with us at our table. After everybody was settled, we proceeded to introduce ourselves to them and invite them to come to our Healing Crusade. I had to explain to the women what the Healing Crusade was all about. One woman exclaimed afterwards, "I was expecting that all of us at this table would have a great time tonight but now I'm really very disappointed," she said, laughing and joking at the same time. Seven women told us that they could not come because they had to work on those days. "No work, no money, as you know," the women told us. Three women informed us that they may be able to come for only one day, because it was their day off.

"The Lord can do a lot of healings and miracles even in a blink of an eye," I told the women. "Just come and see," I further assured them.

Sure enough, these three women came to St. Mary's Church during the second day of the Healing Crusade, and they introduced themselves to me again. I was able to pray with them and ministered to them. I deeply felt the Lord's overwhelming love and compassion for them, and He manifested His love through the gifts of the word of prophecy, words of knowledge, and healing that the Holy Spirit had worked through me. The women were deeply touched by the Lord, glory to God, and they could not thank me enough for ministering to them in the mighty Name of Jesus.

Indeed, the Lord has many amazing and pleasant surprises for His children, alleluia!

In June 2003, the Alliance of the Filipino Catholic Charismatic Prayer Communities in North America (AFCCPC), in which I serve as the Overall National

Coordinator to this day, held a National Convention in the Hilton Hotel in New Brunswick, New Jersey.

After the three-day convention, a leadership meeting was held in the hotel.

Before the start of the meeting, Dr. Al Albarracin, from Columbus, Ohio, a member of the AFCCPC Board at that time, and I were trading jokes with each other. I had a very hearty laugh, I remember. The next thing I knew, I was being transported into a hospital room. Dr. Joe Nepomuceno from Baltimore, Maryland, also an AFCCPC officer at that time, rode with me in the ambulance. He told me, "Bob, in the ambulance, you kept on singing, 'With Jesus in my vessel, I can smile at the storm.' You sang it non-stop since we left the Hotel." I told him that I could not remember a thing that happened to me, although I remember that Dr. Albarracin and I were laughing heartily.

Dr. Joe told me that I suddenly dropped on the floor while I was still laughing. "Bob, you gave all of us a big scare. We all thought you had a heart attack. Everybody is praying for you."

"Joe, by the way, how did I sound like when I was singing in the ambulance non-stop?" I asked Dr. Nepomuceno. "I didn't remember a thing of what happened to me. You know, we have not sung that song, 'With Jesus in My Vessel, I can Smile at the Storm' in the prayer meeting at St. Luke's for a long, long time," I told Joe. "It must have been the Holy Spirit who was singing through me," I opined. "Don't worry, Bob, you sounded like Frank Sinatra," he retorted back to me with a big smile on his face.

The doctor's diagnosis? The attending physician at the Robert Johnson Wood Hospital in New Brunswick,

New Jersey, told me that I probably had a vasovagal syncope episode. Vasovagal syncope is a condition that leads to fainting in some people. It is the most common cause of fainting. It's usually not harmful nor a sign of a more serious problem. Many nerves connect with your heart and blood vessels. Vasovagal syncope causes the heart rate and the blood pressure to drop suddenly.

The attending physician had decided to keep me overnight in the hospital and he also scheduled me to be released in the early morning hours the following day.

At 4:00 A.M., a nurse woke me up. She said, "Some nurses on this floor know you. They said you are very active in the Healing ministry. Is it okay with you if you could pray over some of us before you go home?" I said to her, "Sure, it would be my pleasure to do so." "How about right now?", she inquired.

I retorted back to her, "Yes, by all means." Then she left the room to call the other nurses.

I then said to the Lord, "Lord you don't have to put me in the hospital for me to minister to these nurses here, but your will be done."

Eight female nurses came into my room, wanting me to pray over them. So I got out of my bed, secured my very loose hospital gown, and positioned my IV pole so that I could lay my hands on them. I asked for two male nurses to come inside the room to catch any of the nurses just in case they would "rest" in the Spirit or fall down on the floor. Then I started to pray over them. Each one of them received a personal prophecy or a personal message from the Holy Spirit plus a word of knowledge about their respective personal situations. All of them fell down to the floor, most of them crying and sobbing. They asked me how did I know about their personal lives and their situations when we only met for the first time. I told them that I was only a mouthpiece for the Holy Spirit, a poor instrument of His. They all told me that they received peace and joy and confidence after they heard their respective messages because, according to them, "the messages were right on." "Now we know for sure that the Lord loves us and that we can rely on Him no matter what," they further told me. Most, if not all of them, also informed me that they were healed of various aches and pains in their bodies. Glory to God!

If someone would ask me what is the best of the gifts of the Holy Spirit to manifest or to exercise, I would venture to say that the best spiritual gift is the gift that is most needed and the most appropriate in a particular situation and at a particular time. For instance, if someone is sick and needs healing, then of course, the gift of healing is the most needed gift. If a person needs direction on how to live a Godly life, then the gift of the word of wisdom and the word of knowledge and prophecy would be the most appropriate gifts to use in this situation.

If a person is terminally ill or in a very precarious situation, the best gifts that are needed are, of course, the gift of healing and the gift of miracles.

If someone is speaking in tongues during a prayer meeting or prayer assembly, then the best charisms that are appropriate to use are the gifts of discernment of spirits and the gift of interpretation of tongues and, to some degree, the gift of prophecy so that everyone can understand the message that is being given in tongues.

St. Paul says in 1 Corinthians 1:7, "...so that you are not lacking in any spiritual gift as you wait for the revelation of our Lord Jesus Christ."

I encourage everyone to ask the Lord to pour out the charisms of the Holy Spirit on you.

Jesus says in Matthew 7:7–11:

> Ask and it will be given to you; seek and you will find; knock and the door will be opened to you. For everyone who asks, receives; and the one who seeks, finds; and to the one who knocks, the door will be opened. Which one of you would hand his son a stone when he asks for a loaf of bread, or a snake when he asks for a fish? If you then, who are wicked, know how to give good gifts to your children, how much more will your heavenly Father give good things to those who ask him.

I asked the Holy Spirit to pour out upon me all the spiritual gifts in their full measures, not for my vain glory or for any selfish reason, but for me to serve Him well by serving my fellow human beings in His name for His glory and honor. I consider it a great privilege indeed and a great honor and blessing for me personally to be able to minister to a fellow human being in need of hope, and peace, and healing in the Name of Jesus. Not everyone is afforded this blessing and privilege. It is like music to my ears if someone says to me, "Because of what you did, my life has become more bearable and easier to live, and I have become closer to the Lord Jesus."

Without hesitation, I have asked the Lord and I keep asking Him to be with me always because I need Him badly. For without the Lord, I am nothing and I cannot do anything for His honor and glory. Furthermore, I ask Him also to let the fruit of the Holy Spirit really blossom in my life, because without the fruit of the Holy Spirit, even if I had all the gifts, it is impossible for me or for anyone else for that matter, to enter into His Kingdom. Come, Lord Jesus, Come.

Robert speaking on "How to Receive and Use the Mighty Power of the Holy Spirit." Church of the Ascension, Elmhurst, Queens, New York, November 2018.

Robert calling out healings using the spiritual gift of the Word of Knowledge before a church-packed congregation.

Chapter 2 Endnote

1. LG 12 # 2; cf. AA 3.

CHAPTER 3
The Fruit
that Will Last

What is the fruit that will last? Actually, I am talking about the fruit of the Holy Spirit.

The fruit of the Holy Spirit is produced by the Holy Spirit, not by the Christian. The Greek word is singular, showing that "fruit" is a unified whole, not independent characteristics. As we grow closer to the Lord and walk with Him, hopefully all the characteristics of Christ will manifest in our lives.

In Galatians 5:22–25, St. Paul asserts:

> …the fruit of the Spirit is love, joy, peace, patience, kindness, generosity, faithfulness, gentleness, self-control. Against such there is no law. Now those who belong to Christ [Jesus] have crucified their flesh with its passions and desires. If we live in the Spirit, let us also follow the Spirit.

A so-called "fruit of the evil one" also exists. In Galatians 5:19–21, St. Paul says:

> Now the works of the flesh are obvious: immorality, impurity, licentiousness, idolatry, sorcery, hatreds, rivalry, jealousy, outbursts of fury, acts of selfishness, dissensions, factions, occasions of envy, drinking bouts, orgies, and the like. I warn you, as I warned you before, that those who do such things will not inherit the kingdom of God.

To possess the fruit of the Holy Spirit, is to possess the character of Jesus in our lives. The fruit of the Holy Spirit is our so-called "passport" or "passageway" into the Kingdom of God.

Jesus says in Matthew 7:21-23:

> Not everyone who says to me, "Lord, Lord," will enter the kingdom of heaven, but only the one who does the will of my Father in heaven. Many will say to me on that day, "Lord, Lord, did we not prophesy in your name? Did we not drive out demons in your name? Did we not do mighty deeds in your name?" Then I will declare to them solemnly, "I never knew you. Depart from me, you evildoers."

It should be noted that Jesus, in this scripture passage, did not deny that these people who prophesied and cast out demons or performed miracles did so in His name. He was emphasizing the fact that those who walk in holiness and those who have the character of Christ, or the fruit of the Holy Spirit, are His true disciples and followers and, therefore, are the ones who will inherit God's Kingdom.

Jesus did not devalue or diminish or lessen the importance of the gifts of the Spirit in this scripture passage, but He was saying a person who does the will of the Heavenly Father, he who walks in holiness, will possess life eternal. It is our Heavenly Father's desire to shape and mold us into the image and likeness of His Son, our Lord Jesus Christ. All we need to do is open ourselves up to the power of the Holy Spirit working in our lives.

The fruit of the Holy Spirit takes some time to fully develop and grow and mature within us. When we give our lives to Jesus, surrender to His will, walk with Him, fellowship with Him, and follow Him on a daily basis, chances are we will become more like Him.

The manifestation of the fruit of the Spirit in our lives is a sure and hard evidence that we are being imbued with the character of our Lord Jesus Christ.

In Colossians 3:12–14, St. Paul declares:

> Put on then, as God's chosen ones, holy and beloved, heartfelt compassion, kindness, humility, gentleness, and patience, bearing with one another and forgiving one another, if one has a grievance against another; as the Lord has forgiven you, so must you also do. And over all these put on love, that is, the bond of perfection.

The Catechism of the Catholic Church #1824 and #1825, states as follows:

> Fruit of the Spirit and fullness of the Law, charity keeps the *commandments* of God and

his Christ: "Abide in my love. If you keep my commandments, you will abide in my love."[1] Christ died out of love for us, while we were still "enemies."[2] The Lord asks us to love as he does, even our *enemies*, to make ourselves the neighbor of those farthest away, and to love children and the poor as Christ himself.[3]

"The *fruits* of the Spirit are perfections that the Holy Spirit forms in us as the first fruits of eternal glory." (CCC #1832)

Love, according to St. Paul, is the only fruit of the Holy Spirit that lasts because each fruit depends on love for it to exist. Love, therefore, must be the underlying reason for us in exercising the spiritual gifts: the love of God and the love for God's people. Love is the key that opens the Kingdom of Heaven.

Read in its entirety what St. Paul declares in 1 Corinthians 13:1–13:

> If I speak in human and angelic tongues but do not have love, I am a resounding gong or a clashing cymbal. And if I have the gift of prophecy and comprehend all mysteries and all knowledge; if I have all faith so as to move mountains but do not have love, I am nothing. If I give away everything I own, and if I hand my body over so that I may boast but do not have love, I gain nothing.
>
> Love is patient, love is kind. It is not jealous, [love] is not pompous, it is not inflated, it is not rude, it does not seek its own interests, it is not

quick-tempered, it does not brood over injury, it does not rejoice over wrongdoing but rejoices with the truth. It bears all things, believes all things, hopes all things, endures all things.

Love never fails. If there are prophecies, they will be brought to nothing; if tongues, they will cease; if knowledge, it will be brought to nothing. For we know partially and we prophesy partially, but when the perfect comes, the partial will pass away. When I was a child, I used to talk as a child, think as a child, reason as a child; when I became a man, I put aside childish things. At present we see indistinctly, as in a mirror, but then face to face. At present I know partially; then I shall know fully, as I am fully known. So faith, hope, love remain, these three; but the greatest of these is love.

How to Develop the Fruit of the Spirit in Our Life

In Galatians 5:16, St. Paul instructs us: "I say, then: live by the Spirit and you will certainly not gratify the desire of the flesh." In verse 18, St. Paul says: "But if you are guided by the Spirit, you are not under the law."

Furthermore, in Galatians 5:24–25, St. Paul advises:

> Now those who belong to Christ [Jesus] have crucified their flesh with its passions and desires. If we live in the Spirit, let us also follow the Spirit.

One of my prayers every day is for the fruit of the Holy Spirit to blossom in my life and for the Lord to pour out upon me His spiritual gifts in spite of myself so that I will become an "effective worker in His vineyard."

Wherever and whenever the gifts of the Holy Spirit are exercised in love and compassion, signs and wonders and healings and miracles will always be there. In Acts 3:1–10, the Word of God says:

> Now Peter and John were going up to the temple area for the three o'clock hour of prayer. And a man crippled from birth was carried and placed at the gate of the temple called "the Beautiful Gate" every day to beg for alms from the people who entered the temple. When he saw Peter and John about to go into the temple, he asked for alms. But Peter looked intently at him, as did John, and said, "Look at us." He paid attention to them, expecting to receive something from them. Peter said, "I have neither silver nor gold, but what I do have I give you: in the name of Jesus Christ the Nazorean, [rise and] walk." Then Peter took him by the right hand and raised him up, and immediately his feet and ankles grew strong. He leaped up, stood, and walked around, and went into the temple with them, walking and jumping and praising God. When all the people saw him walking and praising God, they recognized him as the one who used to sit begging at the Beautiful Gate of the temple, and they were filled with amazement and astonishment at what had happened to him.

Back in November 1997, I had the privilege to minister in my late father's former hometown church, Santa Teresa De Avila in Talisay, Cebu, Philippines. The church was packed to capacity. By the entrance of the church, I caught sight of a woman lying on a cot and a man standing by her who, I found out, was her husband. I went to talk to them, and the man told me that his wife had cancer. He said she could not walk also because of the cancer in her body. I really felt so much pity and compassion for her, that I said to the Lord on my way inside the Church: "Lord, even if you would only heal one person, and this person is that woman by the entrance of the church, it would be more than enough for me."

During the Healing Service, many people received their healing, including the blind and the deaf, and the oppressed by evil spirits were set free by the Lord Jesus. When I commanded the paralyzed to stand up and walk in Jesus' Name, many left their wheelchairs behind and started walking towards the altar. The last persons walking toward the altar were the woman by the entrance of the Church and her husband. My heart was dancing with joy and awe while watching her walk. The Lord had answered the desires of my heart! In Psalm 37:4, God's words say: "Delight yourself in the Lord; and He will give you the desires of your heart."

Can you imagine the awesome and mighty power that would be working through us if and when the Holy Spirit possesses us entirely; our will, our heart, our mind, our body, our spirit, our senses, our entire being? That could only be possible if we surrender ourselves to the Holy Spirit to be guided by the Holy Spirit, controlled by the Holy Spirit, filled with the Holy Spirit, anointed by the Holy Spirit, led by the Holy Spirit, used by the

Holy Spirit, and able to minister through the power of the Holy Spirit.

Jesus, in His humanity, experienced and did all of these things. Of course, for us, this does not happen overnight. We need abundant grace from God to live like Jesus lived. We have to continually keep our hearts, minds, and eyes fixed on Jesus, the leader and perfecter of faith. (cf. Hebrews 12:2)

In Colossians 3:5–6, 12–13, St. Paul says:

> Put to death, then, the parts of you that are earthly: immorality, impurity, passion, evil desire, and the greed that is idolatry. Because of these the wrath of God is coming [upon the disobedient].

> Put on then, as God's chosen ones, holy and beloved, heartfelt compassion, kindness, humility, gentleness, and patience, bearing with one another and forgiving one another, if one has a grievance against another; as the Lord has forgiven you, so must you also do.

Chapter 3 Endnotes

1. Jn 15:9-10; cf. Mt 22:40; Rom 13:8-10.
2. Rom 5:10.
3. Cf. Mt 5:44; Lk 10:27-37; Mk 9:37; Mt 25:40, 45.

INTELLECTUAL GIFTS

CHAPTER 4
The Gift
of the Word of Wisdom

"To one is given through the Spirit the expression of wisdom; . . ."
— *1 Cor. 12:8* —

Word of Wisdom—The gift by which the Holy Spirit directs a person to make the right decision or judgment and to live a true Christian life.

Generally, most Catholics acknowledge this gift by praying for the Light of the Spirit. It is a supernatural perspective to ascertain the divine means of accomplishing God's will in a given situation. A person, through the unction of the Holy Spirit, is empowered to give practical, active, or directive teaching, which is an instrument of God for the receivers or hearers.

One good example that demonstrates the gift of the Word of Wisdom is found in 1 Kings 3:16–28.

King Solomon, whom the Lord had lavished with the gift of wisdom, was called upon to solve the dispute between two women who claimed to be the mother of a child.

> Later, two prostitutes came to the king and stood before him. One woman said: "By your leave, my lord, this woman and I live in the same house, and I gave birth in the house while she was present. On the third day after I gave birth, this woman also gave birth. We were alone; no one else was in the house with us; only the two of us were in the house. This woman's son died during the night when she lay on top of him. So, in the middle of the night, she got up and took my son from my side, as your servant was sleeping. Then she laid him in her bosom and laid her dead son in my bosom. I rose in the morning to nurse my son, and he was dead! But when I examined him in the morning light, I saw it was not the son I had borne." The other woman answered, "No! The living one is my son, the dead one is yours." But the first kept saying, "No! the dead one is your son, the living one is mine!" Thus, they argued before the king. Then the king said: "One woman claims, 'This, the living one, is my son, the dead one is yours.' The other answers, 'No! The dead one is your son, the living one is mine.'" The king continued, "Get me a sword." When they brought the sword before the king, he said, "Cut the living child in two, and give half to one woman and half to the other." The woman whose son was alive, because she

was stirred with compassion for her son, said to the king, "Please, my lord, give her the living baby—do not kill it!" But the other said, "It shall be neither mine nor yours. Cut it in two!" The king then answered, "Give her the living baby! Do not kill it! She is the mother." When all Israel heard the judgment the king had given, they were in awe of him, because they saw that the king had in him the wisdom of God for giving right judgment.

In many instances in the scriptures, and in normal life situations of the time, Jesus used words of wisdom to minister and teach about the Kingdom of God. In Luke 18:20–22, it reads:

"…You know the commandments, 'You shall not commit adultery; you shall not kill; you shall not steal; you shall not bear false witness; honor your father and your mother.'" And he replied, "All of these I have observed from my youth." When Jesus heard this he said to him, "There is still one thing left for you: sell all that you have and distribute it to the poor, and you will have a treasure in heaven. Then come, follow me."

In Luke 5:4–10, it reads:

After he had finished speaking, he said to Simon, "Put out into deep water and lower your nets for a catch." Simon said in reply, "Master, we have worked hard all night and have caught nothing, but at your command I will lower the nets." When they had done this, they caught a great number of fish and their nets were tearing. They signaled to their partners in the other boat to come to help them. They came and filled both boats so that they were in danger of sinking. When Simon Peter saw this, he fell at the knees of Jesus and said, "Depart from me, Lord, for I am a sinful man." For astonishment at the catch of fish they had made seized him and all those with him, and likewise James and John, the sons of Zebedee, who were partners of Simon. Jesus said to Simon, "Do not be afraid; from now on you will be catching men."

In Matthew 22:15–22, we read an account where Jesus also demonstrated the words of wisdom in front of the Pharisees.

Then the Pharisees went off and plotted how they might entrap him in speech. They sent their disciples to him, with the Herodians, saying, "Teacher, we know that you are a truthful man and that you teach the way of God in accordance with the truth. And you are not concerned with anyone's opinion, for you do not regard a person's status. Tell us, then, what is your opinion: Is it lawful to pay the census tax to Caesar or not?" Knowing their malice, Jesus said, "Why are you testing me, you hypocrites? Show me the coin that pays the census tax." Then they handed him the Roman coin.

THE GIFT OF THE WORD OF WISDOM

> He said to them, "Whose image is this and whose inscription?" They replied, "Caesar's." At that he said to them, "Then repay to Caesar what belongs to Caesar and to God what belongs to God." When they heard this they were amazed, and leaving him they went away.

The apostles and disciples of Jesus also used the word of wisdom given to them by the Holy Spirit.

In Acts 15:27–29, we read:

> So we are sending Judas and Silas who will also convey this same message by word of mouth: 'It is the decision of the holy Spirit and of us not to place on you any burden beyond these necessities, namely, to abstain from meat sacrificed to idols, from blood, from meats of strangled animals, and from unlawful marriage. If you keep free of these, you will be doing what is right. Farewell.'"

On some occasions, I have also experienced using the word of wisdom that I believe the Holy Spirit has gifted to me, especially during the time of ministry.

One day, a lady came up to me outside of St. Mary's Church in downtown Stockton, California, after I attended Mass one Monday afternoon. She requested that I pray over her because she "felt that evil spirits had been attacking her." She told me that she had been experiencing fear, anxiety, depression, insomnia, and unexplained anger. She further said, "No doubt, evil spirits are the cause of all of these." So, I prayed over her. While praying over her, I sensed that the Lord was directing me to ask her to see a doctor. "I believe what you are experiencing is being caused by hormonal imbalances." "Are you sure?", she asked me. "Yes! I pray that your doctor will give you the correct diagnosis and that he will give you the correct prescriptions," was my reply to her. "As you know, doctors and other medical professionals, including medications, are also being used by the Lord to heal," I further stated.

A month later, I saw the lady again outside of St. Mary's Church, and she told me that the doctor had confirmed that she had hormonal imbalance. She said that the symptoms she had been suffering from had disappeared after she had started taking the medications that her doctor had prescribed for her.

A testimony that I received not too long ago, plus others, have indicated that the gift of the word of wisdom was operative during Healing Rallies.

Testimonials About The Word of Wisdom

Dear Bob Canton,

At one of the conferences I attended in New Jersey sometime in 2010, I asked God if He was truly working through you. I wanted proof of this. I asked God in my prayer to confirm it. As I walked up to the line for healing and when it was my turn, Bob, all of a sudden, told me everything about myself and what I had been through. He said that I was addicted to drugs and was healed of it, that I went to Medjugorje, and a lot of other things God would only know about me and nobody else. I had never met or talked to Mr. Canton before. He told me I still had a spirit of addiction above me. He prayed and told me he bound and rebuked it in Jesus' Name and cast it to the foot of the Cross of Jesus. I asked God to forgive me for my unbelief and for being a doubting Thomas.

Thank you, God, for working miracles through brother Bob Canton. I am a believer that You are working through this holy man of God. And Bob, I was amazed at the healing of my 90-year-old mother-in-law, Frances Sheridan, at the August 19–20, 2016, Catholic Charismatic Conference in Washington Township, New Jersey.

You told my mother-in-law that the Lord was doing an "overhaul" on her. Jesus healed her eyesight and her deafness the very moment you prayed over her in the presence of hundreds of people, including some priests, and she is walking better through you, Bob, by the power of Jesus. She has no more sunglasses inside the house or anywhere. The light doesn't bother her eyes anymore. She is happy she can see and read the paper now. We, her relatives, do not have to talk real loud for her to hear us. She can hear loud and clear now. She looks much younger now with a glow on her face. She was dancing at the conference after she was healed of leg problems. She could even lift her legs high now.

AMAZING. I hope that woman I met who told me she had a video of my mother-in-law walking normally and dancing with gusto will send a copy to you. The day after, my mother-in-law told me in a joking way, "I wish I had asked Bob to ask God for a new set of teeth for me and to make me look twenty years younger." God really did an overhaul on Frances, my 90-year-old mother-in-law.

Thanks, Bob. Much peace and love through Jesus and Mary,
John B. Mastrobuono
New Jersey

P.S. Thank you, Mr. Canton, for saying "Yes" to God.

Dear Bob Canton,

In March 2012, I had a sinus infection in my right nostril. It started with a persistent leakage of pus followed by painful congestion in my forehead, eye, and cheek areas. My condition gradually worsened as I was not responding to the numerous antibiotics and prescription medications I was taking.

All praise and thanks to our merciful God, nasal cancer was ruled out after a series of tests and scans.

In February the following year, I had to undergo surgery for the condition which, by this time, had become chronic sinusitis. However, a month after the surgery, I was no better. My nostril was still leaking pus, I was still changing antibiotics, was put on steroids, and visiting the doctor weekly to drain out the pus.

My case was eventually assigned to a Professor-Doctor at the hospital. He expressed surprise that I was still not well and made changes to my medications yet again. By this time, I was miserable and frustrated that all the medications I had been taking were not working on me. The leakage had become extremely profuse and my nose was sore from the endless blowing and wiping it had been subjected to. Seeing me so, my sister felt I needed divine healing and encouraged me to attend your April 19, 2013, Healing Rally, which was being held in my parish at the Church of the Risen Christ in Toa Payoh, Singapore, and I looked forward to it. It so happened that I saw the Professor-Doctor on April 18, and he put me on new antibiotics for a two-week course.

I started my new antibiotics on the morning of April 19, and was devastated I wasn't going to make it to your healing rally that night when I suffered from gastritis and nausea. In the evening, my sister asked if I was attending the rally, and I told her about the side effects of the medications I was experiencing.

Later on, she told me that during the rally, attended by some two thousand-plus, you announced that the Lord was healing people with sinus infections and that you prayed for those with sinus infections. My sister stood in for me. This is what you told her: "Tell your sister to thank the Lord for what He is doing right now, for nothing is impossible for God." That night at home, I prayed that Jesus would touch me and all who had come to your rally with His healing hand.

The next day, the leakage had subsided considerably. Then suddenly on that same evening, I felt air passing through my right nostril, and the thought came to me that my nostril was dry and I was healed! When I blew my nose and absolutely nothing came out, it was such a profound moment for me as I fell to my knees exclaiming, "My Lord and my God! Thank You, Jesus for healing me and freeing me from this chronic condition!" A great weight was lifted off my shoulders, and I was filled with unbelievable joy and peace.

When I was examined on May 2, the Professor-Doctor was amazed at my incredible recovery and commented that my sinuses looked so normal; it was as if I never ever had a sinus problem at all. He said he just did not have an explanation for it.

God bless you, Bob Canton, and your Healing Ministry, and may the Holy Spirit continue to empower you as you minister (whether conveniently or inconveniently) to people all over the world. It's been seven weeks since I was miraculously healed, and joy is still bubbling over in my heart! We are looking forward to your coming back to Singapore next year. We would also like to attend your Healing Crusades in New Zealand and in Tasmania with some of our relatives three months from now. Praise the Lord! How great indeed is our God!

Agnes Lee
Singapore

Dear Bob Canton,
I had suffered from severe bursitis and carpal tunnel syndrome in my left arm for a long time. My arm was very painful and I could not use it completely. I took pain killer medications and I also had cortisone injections to ease the excruciating pain. I also had been wearing an arm brace. Then I decided to call you by phone and requested you to pray for me for healing. Three days later, my doctor had confirmed that my bursitis and carpal tunnel syndrome were totally healed.

According to my doctor, my affected left arm was stronger than my right arm. This I found to be a miracle from our Lord Jesus. The pain in my left arm is gone and I do not wear my arm brace anymore! I have complete use of my arm now, praise the Lord!

Thanks also for your advice that I believe was coming from the Holy Spirit that it is comforting to forgive our enemies. I have decided to forgive and now I feel free. I am very happy to learn and to realize that the Lord knows all of our thoughts and desires and events and happenings and undertakings in our life. Thanks for the enlightenment and words of wisdom that you have imparted to me. I am now very content by all the graces that the Lord has given me and my family. There are plenty of them!

I see things now in a very different perspective, in the perspective through the guidance of the Holy Spirit. I now realize that if we focus our eyes on the Lord Jesus Christ, we can always withstand all our hardships and trials, because He is always there to give us the strength and the wisdom and guidance and grace that we need.

Jesus is alive and He is the Divine Healer, and miracles are still happening in this day and age. We should trust in His love and compassion for all of us.

I thank the Lord Jesus for letting me experience His power and His presence. Certainly, our God is at work in our lives.

Your sister in Christ Jesus,

Erotida D. Lao

So. San Francisco, CA

Prayer for Receiving and Using the Gift of the Word of Wisdom

Holy Spirit, the Giver of all Gifts,
I ask you to grant me the gift
of the word of wisdom
in the mighty Name of Jesus.
I believe that nothing is impossible
with you. Use me to build up
the faith of people around me,
in your loving and saving,
and healing power.
Let your wisdom be upon me
so that I will be able to follow your
ways and help those who are lost to
be able to know you and follow you
for your greater glory and honor.
I ask this in Jesus' Name, Amen.

INTELLECTUAL GIFTS

CHAPTER 5
The Gift
of the Word of Knowledge

"...to another the expression
of knowledge according
to the same Spirit;"
— 1 Cor. 12:8 —

Word of Knowledge—A tiny portion of God's total knowledge supernaturally imparted by the Holy Spirit.

Like a word of wisdom, supernatural knowledge doesn't come by natural reasoning, training, or education, but directly by the Holy Spirit. It is operated only under God's control.

The word of knowledge also falls under the category of the Intellectual Gifts. It is simply the Holy Spirit transmitting His specific knowledge to someone about something that this person has no ability or means to be able to know about with his own limited knowledge and wisdom. A great demonstration of the the gift of the word of knowledge in the Old Testament was through the prophet Elisha who was endowed by God with super-natural knowledge of various things.

In the book of 2 Kings 5:10–14, we read about Naaman, the captain of the Syrian army, who heard that there was a man of God from Israel through whom he would be healed of his leprosy.

> Elisha sent him the message: "Go and wash seven times in the Jordan, and your flesh will heal, and you will be clean." But Naaman went away angry, saying, "I thought that he would surely come out to me and stand there to call on the name of the LORD his God, and would move his hand over the place, and thus cure the leprous spot. Are not the rivers of Damascus, the Abana and the Pharpar, better than all the waters of Israel? Could I not wash in them and be cleansed?" With this, he turned about in anger and left.

> But his servants came up and reasoned with him: "My father, if the prophet told you to do something extraordinary, would you not do it? All the more since he told you, 'Wash, and be clean'?" So Naaman went down and plunged into the Jordan seven times, according to the word of the man of God. His flesh became again like the flesh of a little child, and he was clean.

In the Gospel of John, we read about Jesus using this powerful word of knowledge that changed and transformed lives of many.

One day, Jesus was conversing with a woman who turned out to be one of the "greatest evangelists," I believe, in the time of Jesus after she conversed with Him. We read in John 4:16-19:

> Jesus said to her, "Go call your husband and come back." The woman answered and said to him, "I do not have a husband." Jesus answered her, "You are right in saying, 'I do not have a husband.' For you have had five husbands, and the one you have now is not your husband. What you have said is true." The woman said to him, "Sir, I can see that you are a prophet."

John 4:39 says:

> Many of the Samaritans of that town began to believe in him because of the word of the woman who testified, "He told me everything I have done."

Jesus is truly God and truly man. But in His humanity, He had to rely on the power of the Holy Spirit to do and say what He did and to reveal truths to people such as the Samaritan woman by the well.

Acts 9:10–16, tells a story about Ananias who was endowed by the Lord with a powerful word of knowledge to save the life and ministry of St. Paul.

> There was a disciple in Damascus named Ananias, and the Lord said to him in a vision, "Ananias." He answered, "Here I am,

Lord." The Lord said to him, "Get up and go to the street called Straight and ask at the house of Judas for a man from Tarsus named Saul. He is there praying, and [in a vision] he has seen a man named Ananias come in and lay [his] hands on him, that he may regain his sight." But Ananias replied, "Lord, I have heard from many sources about this man, what evil things he has done to your holy ones in Jerusalem. And here he has authority from the chief priests to imprison all who call upon your name." But the Lord said to him, "Go, for this man is a chosen instrument of mine to carry my name before Gentiles, kings, and Israelites, and I will show him what he will have to suffer for my name."

The gift of the word of knowledge, in fact, all of the spiritual gifts from the Holy Spirit, have the power and the effects to change the course of the life of a person or people or the entire nation or the entire world or the entire history of the world for that matter.

I humbly say that my life has been profoundly changed because of the Lord Jesus' mercy and love and revelations and empowerments that I have received and have been receiving in my life.

How Do We Receive
The Gift of the Word of Knowledge?

The Lord deals with individuals individually.

Each individual is unique, and no two persons are exactly alike, even identical twins. Scientists have shown that identical twins have very similar DNA when they are born, but as they age, the marks in their DNA become more different.

These are the various ways the Holy Spirit conveys to me the word of knowledge:

1. Through vision or mental picture

These happened many times while I was ministering to God's people.

One time, I was conducting a Healing Service in St. James Church in McMinnville, Oregon. As I led the attendees to pray the "Forgiveness Prayer," I received a vision through the gift of the word of knowledge of a woman who was threatened by an angry man with a gun. He was pointing the gun at her. This man clicked the trigger of the gun, but the trigger had jammed, enabling the woman to escape death.

Furthermore, the Holy Spirit had impressed upon me that this woman had been suffering from fear and depression. When I announced this vision to the attendees, a lady came up crying and sobbing uncontrollably, and she acknowledged that she was that woman.

Then, I received words of prophecy or a message from the Lord for her. The Lord told her, "My daughter, I was there with you and I caused the trigger of the gun not to function. I love you my daughter and I'm always with you. I want you to forgive the man who did this to you. Forgive him from your heart. I'm healing you my daughter and the more you forgive, the more healing you will receive. Remember my daughter, I have forgiven you and I want you to do likewise. I love you my daughter, and I will never abandon you." Thereafter, I prayed for healing of memories and inner healing and for her to receive peace from the Holy Spirit.

No doubt, this lady received emotional, physical, psychological, and mental healings that day.

In John 8:36, the Word of God says: "So if a son frees you, then you will truly be free."

On one occasion, my brother Leo and my sister-in-law Luz were about to leave for San Francisco International Airport to board their flight to Manila, Philippines. I received a frantic call from my brother Leo requesting that my wife Chita and I pray for them to find their airline tickets. Leo said to me, "We are about to leave for San Francisco Airport and we looked all over the place in our house to find our airline tickets. Kindly help us pray. We don't want to miss our flight. We only have three hours left to spare, and it would take us one and one-half hours to drive to San Francisco, as you know."

I hung up and began asking the Holy Spirit to guide Leo and Luz where to find their tickets. I also prayed in tongues under my breath. Then the Holy Spirit gave me a vision of the tickets underneath the crocheted tablecloth on the dresser in their master bedroom.

I called Leo right away and told him about my vision. Leo called back, praising the Lord, telling me that he found the tickets exactly where I described them to be.

God is really good! Incidentally, my brother Leo was ordained a Deacon of the Catholic Church in 2018. Deacon Leo and his wife Luz have been leading a Charismatic Prayer Group at St. George's Parish in Stockton, California, since 1997.

In various instances, through a mental picture, I would see an "ailing" heart or malfunctioning lungs or liver or organs of the body that the Lord is healing at that moment. I will then announce this vision with words from the Lord. Oftentimes, through the promptings of the

Holy Spirit, I would also pray over the sick for complete healing and restoration.

2. Through the voice of the Lord being received in my inner being

In other words, I receive the word of knowledge through the ears of my heart.

Sometimes, the Lord would give me names of people, followed by prophetic words, and/or healing or admonition or affirmation or comfort with the purpose of strengthening their faith and building them up and drawing them closer to the Lord.

3. Through "aches and pains" in my body

Indeed, the Lord works in mysterious ways.

Sometimes while ministering healing to God's people, I would suddenly experience pain on any part of my body. After I announce that the Lord is healing someone with that particular physical problem or pain, and someone would acknowledge the healing, the pain in my body would also vanish immediately.

I have compiled some testimonies that showcase the operation of the gift of the word of knowledge through the power of the Holy Spirit. These testimonies are only a few of many that I have received over the years.

**Testimonials
About the The Word of Knowledge**

Dear Bob Canton:

We have met during the Northern California Charismatic Catholic Convention, which was held in the Santa Clara Convention Center. My mom had not walked for over five years. She fell twice and she broke her femur bone during one fall. Because of the severity of her conditions, she had had surgery twice. However, after these surgeries, she had been confined in the wheelchair for all these years. The accidents had affected her so much ,not only physically but emotionally, and probably psychologically as well.

That day when we first met you during the early morning Mass at the Santa Clara Convention Center, I knew something great was going to happen to us, especially to my mother. You haven't even prayed over her yet, and you told me that my mother is going to get out of the wheelchair that day. I was in tears when you told me this because I felt the love of the Lord Jesus all over me.

That afternoon during your workshop, you prayed over my mom and commanded her to stand up and walk in Jesus' Name. When she stood up and started walking from the wheelchair, I could not believe what I was seeing. I almost fainted when she asked you to sit down in her wheelchair and pushed the wheelchair around with you in it! God is really good. How you knew what was going to happen to my mom that day was beyond me. My mom and I shed many tears of joy! Thank you for being obedient to the prompting of the Holy Spirit and for being sensitive to His leadings and anointing.

Sincerely,
Marcy Fong
San Leandro, California

Dear Bob:
During the Kanto Charismatic Conference in Chiba, Japan, a suburb of Tokyo, on September 23-25, 2016, I had witnessed so many healings. The deaf, the blind, the paralytic were able to hear, see, and walked. Some cysts and tumors were gone. This was verified by Dr. Francisco from Okinawa who was present during the conference and examined those people before and after the Healing

Service. He told the people after the Healing Service that he could no longer feel the tumor or cyst that he had examined before the Healing Service took place.

After the Mass last Sunday, September 25, 2016, Bob came to the priests' vesting room together with Haruyo, the Japanese interpreter, to thank all of us seven priests who attended the Conference.

I had Bob Canton pray for healing of my left foot. It was for the after-effect of a bone fracture, and sometimes I would fall down when I would walk. He picked up my two feet while I was sitting down, and he showed me and Haruyo that my left foot was shorter than the other. Then he started praying, asking the Lord to lengthen my left foot, and he also commanded my foot to be the same length as my right foot in the Name of Jesus. To my surprise, my left foot grew out. It was the first time that I had witnessed something like this. I felt a change immediately. I walked around inside the room without any pain. Since then, my left foot steps straight forward in the same way as the right foot. Every day I am able to walk normally. My body doesn't turn to the left anymore, and I have not fallen down when I walk ever since then.

As Bob was praying over me for my healing, he told me that he received a vision of me inside a closet. He asked me if it meant anything to me. I was very surprised why he knew about it. I told him that when I was about ten years old to around thirteen years old, I was sometimes tied up with a rope by either my mother or sometimes by one of the members of my own family, and then they would put me inside a closet in the house and left me in for a long time.

My family told me all the time that I was a bad boy and that they didn't like me. It affected me so deeply that depression had developed twenty years ago. Up until last week, I had taken medicine every day for it. From the time of childhood days, I was convinced that I was loved by God all the time, but at the same time, I felt "all friends" disliked me much. I also felt that most of the priests that I knew looked down on me, and I felt they avoided me when they saw me.

Bob told me that he had a vision of Jesus with me all the time when I was imprisoned inside the closet. He said Jesus was crying with me inside the closet and that He was holding me and loving me. Bob said that he heard Jesus telling me, "My son, I am with you and I will never leave you. I'm crying here with you my son."

My heart became calm day by day since then, and I feel like something is melting inside of me since Bob prayed over me and told me about his vision. This healing is a precious present for me from our God. Because I am already old, I hate nobody and I forgave my family and I am happy and at peace because I know Jesus loves me and He will never leave me. I feel that the depression is gone and I'm looking forward for more blessings from God.

Thank you, Bob. We will meet in the house of our Master and will always be united in Christ. I would like to see you back in Japan next year as you promised to us.

Fr. Kei Francisco X.
Tokyo, Japan

Hey Bob,

Here are my eye-witness accounts of the healings at St. Peter and All Hallows Parish, on December 15, 2017, in Sacramento.

The Mass and Healing service at St. Peter and All Hallows Parish, with Bob Canton was awesome. Praise the FATHER, JESUS, and the HOLY SPIRIT.

There were healings of people with hearing aids, and they did not need them anymore. People with canes and walkers were healed and did not need their canes or walkers anymore. Two Blind people were healed. It was a mighty move of the HOLY SPIRIT. Probably more we will find out later. Some I know already. I saw these with my own eyes. I witnessed them myself. Let me share just a few.

Bob Canton got a word from the LORD for people with hearing aids to come up to the front. One Lady had two hearing aids, one for each ear and could not hear without them. Bob prayed as the HOLY SPIRIT led him. I personally held the hearing aids. Bob tested for healing by getting behind the Lady and snapping his fingers and telling her to raise her hand if she could hear. She did, and she also repeated sentences that Bob would say to her as well. Bob spoke low as he said these things. This same Lady also had a cane. Bob prayed for Healing in the Name of JESUS, The FATHER and in the HOLY SPIRIT again. Her son was there, and he said that she had to be helped to walk up steps, and people had to get on each side of her so she would not fall because she would wobble. Anyway, she was healed! She not only walked back and forth on the altar but also she ran.

Bob had also mentioned in his talk that unforgiveness is a block to healing. Well, a lady with hearing aids came up for prayers. There was a slight improvement in her hearing after Bob prayed over her. Then Bob got the word of knowledge that she needed to forgive someone, a lady who was a very close relative of hers, and her daughter who stood next to her confirmed it to be so. Her daughter said that her mom needed healing to walk as well. She was up there with some assistance. Bob prayed for her to be able to walk. Well, our merciful LORD healed her, and she walked back and forth with no assistance. All the GLORY to our LORD, the FATHER, JESUS, and the HOLY SPIRIT.

Bob always prays in the Name of JESUS. He prays to and as the HOLY SPIRIT leads him. He prays to our FATHER.

Another lady came up and had a walker and could not walk without it. She also mentioned that her knee could not bend. Bob again prayed over her in Jesus' Name. She walked without the walker. I saw her walking without her walker, but her right leg was still straight. Bob prayed again and asked the LORD that she would be able to bend her knee. Praise the LORD, she was able to bend her knee. She also ran back and forth around the altar.

Bob called up blind people; two came up, with some help of course. One guy had a brain injury. The injury caused the blindness. Bob prayed for healing of the brain and for the eyes. Bob said okay, let's test it, to see if he could see. Bob was a few feet away, and told the guy to do what he would be doing to test his eyesight. Bob raised his own hand up, waving left to right. The guy repeated it. Bob then moved his own right hand to the side, making an up and down motion. The guy repeated it. Bob did the same with the left hand as well, and the guy repeated it.

The other blind guy was healed when he came up as well. Bob prayed over him and he commanded the spirit of blindness to go in Jesus' Name. Afterwards, he was tested too. He told Bob, "I can see, I can see, thank God! This guy was jumping up and down with excitement on his face. I could see that the people were in awe of what they had witnessed.

Bob also prayed with people who had cancer. One lady with cancer was there with her husband and said she felt the presence of the Lord in a very powerful way. Tears of joy were streaming down her eyes. She also asked that Bob pray for her and her husband to be able to have a baby. Bob had mentioned in his book, *Miracles Never Ending,* that there were testimonies from people who could not have babies because of infertility, but later on were healed and were able to get pregnant and have a baby after he had prayed over them.

Bob received a word of knowledge from the LORD for this lady that she would have good news in four months. Praise the LORD! There were more miracles during the healing service. I just shared a few.

All of these show that Jesus heals and that He is a Miracle Worker through the power of the Holy Spirit.

GOD BLESS!

Rod Guidry

Sacramento, California

Dear Bob,

I stood in proxy for my niece during your Healing Service in the Immaculate Heart of Mary Catholic Church in Towson, Maryland. She had been a heroin addict for a long time. As we were praying for her, you received a word of knowledge from the Holy Spirit that my niece would be completely delivered from her addiction by the power of God. Guess what? It has been exactly a year now that my niece has been completely clean from heroin addiction.

Almost a year before you prayed for my niece, I stood in as a proxy for my brother during your Healing Rally at St. John the Evangelist Catholic Church in Severna Park, Maryland. Since then, my brother has come to know the Lord. He was also set free from alcohol and drug addictions. He used to be in a "heavy metal band." Now he plays music for the Lord. He also has joined a Bible study group and has married a born-again Christian. My brother is a completely different person inside by the grace of God. What you said, that "there would be a break-through in his life by the power of the Holy Spirit" when we prayed for him, came to pass. It is true that nothing is impossible for God if we only believe and trust in Him. Thank you for your prayers and for ministering to us in obedience to the Lord Jesus.

God bless you!
Betty Hadricky
Severna Park, Maryland

"Suddenly, an angel of the Lord stood there, and a light shone in the cell. The angel shook Peter by the shoulder, woke him up, and said, 'Hurry! Get up!' At once the chains fell off Peter's hands." (Acts. 12:7)

On January 7, 1999, some members of the Children of God Prayer Community ministered during the Mass and Healing Service at St. John the Baptist Catholic Church in Milpitas, California, sponsored by the Servants of the Good Shepherd prayer group. On our way there, we discovered that one of our headlights was out. After saying the Rosary, we stopped at a gas station. There, all of us in the car prayed for the headlights to work. Praise the Lord! The lights went on, and we continued our journey to Milpitas without anymore trouble. God gave us a preview of what was going to happen.

In his introductory talk, Bob Canton made it clear that Jesus is the Healer, and that we should focus on Him. Then he proceeded to call out the word of knowledge that he received from the Holy Spirit. Before the evening was over, we heard of testimonies from a number of people who saw a light in the church. For one, it was a flashing light. In Acts 12:7, the chains fell of Peter's hands. During the Healing Service, many were set free. Bob was on target with the words of knowledge, especially calling out people by name and also the ailments from which they were healed. Two women, who had been abused by their husbands, received inner healing. Backs and throats were healed. One lady with two bad kidneys felt an intense heat around her body. Another woman had her feet healed. When she offered up her pain to the Lord, she was healed. Depressions were lifted. Bob called out that the Lord was taking out purple body marks and other discolorations from people. Many claimed that their body marks and discolorations were instantly gone. Bob called up a young girl from the congregation and prophecied that she would have a special work in the vineyard of the Lord. She is twelve years old. The atmosphere inside the St. John the Baptist Church was electric.

"The people who live in darkness, will see a great light." (Matthew 4:16)

Fr. Sebastian Drake, O.F.M.

Spiritual Adviser, Children of God Prayer Community

Hello, I'm Stephany Vouakouanitou. I attended your Healing Crusade in St-Leu Paris, France.

For three weeks I had severe headaches and pain around my neck area. It was especially painful that day while I was driving toward the church to attend the Healing Crusade. It was the first time I saw that the St-Leu Church in downtown Paris was very full of people. I even saw some "street walkers," or "women of the street" attending the Healing Crusade. I prayed for them to be healed by the Lord in body, mind, and spirit.

By the way, my dad, Jean Claude, served as the French interpreter for you. After your talk, you called out words of knowledge about people being healed by the Lord of their illnesses. Then you said that you had sensed the Lord healing someone with severe headaches and neck pains.

At first, I didn't expect this healing would concern me, rather it was meant for someone else. Then you pointed your finger at me saying, "You there, the lady who is sitting in the last pew, in the middle of the pew, with a light pink blouse, the Lord Jesus is telling me you are the one."

After you announced this healing, my headaches and my neck pains were gone. In the instant you said those words, the pains were gone! And I gave a testimony in front of the people in the church that the Lord truly healed me. I also praised the name of Jesus, because He is my healer!

Since then, my headaches and my neck pains have never come back.

Merci Jésus!

Stephany Vouakouanitou,

Paris, France

Prayer to Receive the Gift of the Word of Knowledge

Lord Jesus, you are the
Giver of gifts!
All graces and blessings
come from you.
I ask the Holy Spirit to grant me
the gift of the word of knowledge
in Jesus' Name
so that I can become an effective
worker in your vineyard.
Fill me with your Holy Spirit,
oh, Lord,
and use me for your greater glory
and honor.
Thank you, Lord Jesus,
for answering my prayers.
Amen

INTELLECTUAL GIFTS

CHAPTER 6
The Gift of Discernment of Spirits

"...to another discernment
of spirits;...."
—1 Corinthians 12:10—

Discernment of Spirits—Supernatural power
to detect or recognize the realm of the spirits
and their activities.

Another spiritual gift under the category of Intellectual Gifts
is Discernment of Spirits. These are the possible sources of
the manifestations of certain phenomena: the Holy Spirit,
the human spirit, good angels, or demonic spirits.

Very few Christians begin operating in the gifts perfectly the first time. Yet we can practice and "come to
perfection in our understanding and operation of them."

The discernment of spirits is not everyday discernment used for making decisions, nor an insight into human nature that one might naturally possess, nor an ad-
ept ability to suspect something wrong in the motive of
others. It is not the natural ability to assess situations.

The discernment of spirits is a supernatural gift of revelation given for a specific situation. This revelation can come through a vision, a sense, or a specific word similar to a word of knowledge. This manifestation gift requires prayer and maturity in the Spirit.

In short, the gift of discernment of spirits enables a Christian to be a powerful and effective channel of God's wisdom by accurately sensing and knowing a divine or demonic presence in certain people, places, things, and particular phenomena.

An excellent example of the manifestation of this gift is found in Acts 16:16–18:

> As we were going to the place of prayer, we met a slave girl with an oracular spirit, who used to bring a large profit to her owners through her fortune-telling. She began to follow Paul and us, shouting, "These people are slaves of the Most High God, who proclaim to you a way of salvation." She did this for many days. Paul became annoyed, turned, and said to the spirit, "I command you in the name of Jesus Christ to come out of her." Then it came out at that moment.

What the woman with the spirit of the occult said of St. Paul and the other disciples was true. However, St. Paul had discerned that this woman was oppressed by evil spirits.

In the book of Lamentations 2:14, Jeremiah discerns:

> Your prophets provided you visions
>   of whitewashed illusion;

They did not lay bare your guilt,
  in order to restore your fortunes;
They saw for you only oracles
  of empty deceit.

Another account concerns Micaiah, in 1 Kings 22:23, who also discerns evil spirits at work:

So now, the LORD has put a lying spirit in the mouths of all these prophets of yours; the LORD himself has decreed evil against you.

In John 1:47–50, we read,

Jesus saw Nathanael coming toward him and said of him, "Here is a true Israelite. There is no duplicity in him." Nathanael said to him, "How do you know me?" Jesus answered and said to him, "Before Philip called you, I saw you under the fig tree." Nathanael answered him, "Rabbi, you are the Son of God; you are the King of Israel." Jesus answered and said to him, "Do you believe because I told you that I saw you under the fig tree? You will see greater things than this."

Jesus says in Matthew 7:15–18:

Beware of false prophets, who come to you in sheep's clothing, but underneath are ravenous wolves. By their fruits you will know them. Do people pick grapes from thornbushes, or figs from thistles? Just so, every good tree bears good fruit, and a rotten tree bears bad fruit. A good tree cannot bear bad fruit, nor can a rotten tree bear good fruit.

In Matthew 16:21–23, Jesus had discerned that what came out of Peter's mouth when he had learned about the coming passion and death of Jesus was not of God.

From that time on, Jesus began to show his disciples that he must go to Jerusalem and suffer greatly from the elders, the chief priests, and the scribes, and be killed and on the third day be raised. Then Peter took him aside and began to rebuke him, "God forbid, Lord! No such thing shall ever happen to you." He turned and said to Peter, "Get behind me, Satan! You are an obstacle to me. You are thinking not as God does, but as human beings do."

Jesus, obviously, had discerned that Satan was talking through Peter to discourage Him from going through suffering and death on the Cross.

During a Healing Rally that I had the privilege to conduct in St. Brigid Church in Westbury, New York, not too long ago, I prayed over a young woman in her early twenties who was tormented by evil spirits with fear and chronic depression and suicidal tendencies. The lady went down on the floor backwards as I was praying over her. A few minutes later, her body started moving away from the foot of the altar, as if being dragged down by unseen forces, towards the entrance of the Church. She was also making some weird noises and screaming at the same time. I commanded those forces in the Name and by the blood of Jesus to stop dragging her body down the aisle. I discerned that the spirits of divination, fear, heaviness, bondage, and death were tormenting her. I rebuked and commanded all these spirits to leave her in the mighty Name and blood of Jesus and through the power of the Holy Spirit. Her body stopped moving halfway between the altar and the entrance of the Church.

After I recited prayers for healing and deliverance over this young woman, she felt better and very much at peace. I led her into renouncing all these spirits in the Name of Jesus. I also encouraged her to go to Confession at once and to start going to Mass every day without interruption for thirty days. Furthermore, I also encouraged her to recite the Rosary daily and to ask the protection of Mary, the Virgin Mother of God, and St. Joseph and all the angels of heaven, especially Archangel Michael, and to pray in front of the Blessed Sacrament daily, if possible.

This young woman also told me that she had dabbled in the occult, such as playing with tarot cards and Ouija boards. She also had consulted palm readers and fortune tellers. I informed her that the Lord God says in Leviticus 19:31: "Do not go to mediums nor fortune tellers because you will be defiled by them."

If a person opens even a very small door for the evil one to come into his life, the evil one will come in forcefully ready to attack that person with intentions to "kill, steal, and destroy" (cf. John 10:10). Most of the time, evil spirits come in droves. However, Jesus says: "…I came so that they might have life and have it more abundantly" (John 10:10).

Indeed, Jesus is the Divine Healer and Deliverer. The Lord God says in Deuteronomy 18:9–12:

> When you come into the land which the LORD, your God, is giving you, you shall not learn to imitate the abominations of the nations there. Let there not be found among you anyone who causes their son or daughter to pass through the fire, or practices divination, or is a soothsayer, augur, or sorcerer, or who casts spells, consults ghosts and spirits, or seeks oracles from the dead. Anyone who does such things is an abomination to the LORD, and because of such abominations the LORD, your God, is dispossessing them before you.

A few years ago, I had the privilege to conduct Healing Crusades in Sarawak, Kuching, Malaysia, for a second time. I have been to Malaysia at least six times in a period of ten years.

Thousands of people attended our Healing Crusades every time I went to Malaysia.

I can still remember vividly when I came face to face with a man named Valentine. At first I thought that he had an attack of epilepsy because his body was contorting, and he tried to raise his hands with great struggle. Then, I discerned, through the power of the Holy Spirit, that evil spirits were at work in and through him.

Thereafter, I rebuked the spirits of divination, spirits of violence, spirits of afflictions and heaviness, and spirits of anger and hatred. I commanded them to leave and to go to the foot of the Cross to be disposed of by the Lord Jesus and never to come back to molest Valentine or anyone else in the mighty Name and blood of Jesus and through the power of the Holy Spirit. I strongly believe that the angels of God were there in full force to protect God's people and to protect me. Valentine stands about 5'8", and he is brawny and a very muscular person. Had he succeeded in his vile intentions to hit me with his fists, I could just imagine the screaming headlines of the Borneo Post, the daily newspaper in Kuching, Malaysia, the following day, "Kuching Man Knocks Down Healing Evangelist on Church Altar."

Kidding aside, I sincerely believe that I was surrounded and protected by myriad angels.

> Because you have the LORD for your refuge
> and have made the Most High your stronghold,
> No evil shall befall you,
> no affliction come near your tent.
> For he commands his angels with regard to you,
> to guard you wherever you go.
> With their hands they shall support you,
> lest you strike your foot against a stone.
> —Psalm 91:9–12

Every day, I always ask the angels of the Lord, especially Saints Michael, Gabriel, and Raphael and the Archangels, to encamp around my family members, my friends, and all my acquaintances and me for protection and guidance. We have to remember also that Jesus has already won the battle for us against Satan. He won this battle on the Cross at Calvary.

In Romans 8:37, St. Paul says: "...we conquer overwhelmingly through him who loved us."

The Spiritual Gift of Discernment of Spirits is a great tool for ministering to God's people and enables God's people to determine what is from the Holy Spirit, from the human spirit, or from evil spirits.

Our loving Father always desires what is best for us. In James 1:17, the word of God says:

> ...all good giving and every perfect gift is from above, coming down from the Father of lights, with whom there is no alteration or shadow caused by change.

Following is Valentine's amazing testimony that I received from him. Valentine Lim was named as Outstanding Roman Catholic in the Archdiocese of Kuching, Malaysia, in 2018.

Testimonial
About Discernment of Spirits

Dear Mr. Canton,

For ten years, I would follow a group of friends, and we would gather at a small, private Chinese temple. At that time, I was assisting the medium in that Chinese temple.

One evening, when we were attending a birthday celebration of a pagan god at a different Chinese temple, suddenly a foreign spirit entered my body, and I started to behave and act like a monkey. My hands kept on scratching my body and I could not control myself. From that time on, every time I assisted my friend who was a medium in a private temple, a monkey character would start to manifest in me.

Also, for many years, some of my friends and I used to practice "Chee Kung," which involved meditations and exercises to "harness energy within one's body." Then, you came to Kuching, Sarawak, Eastern Malaysia, to conduct Healing Crusades at the Blessed Sacrament Church. I attended the Workshops on Healing during the day and the Healing Services in the evening for four days. I have to tell you, that the very first time I saw you, I was very angry at you. Something inside of me really wanted to hurt you, so I studied your every move. I noticed that you always asked people to form a line so that you could pray over them before the end of every session. So, I planned to hit you with my fists the moment you came face to face with me.

So, when the time came that you were in front of me, the evil spirits began to manifest through me. I tried with all my might to lift up my hands to hit you on the face with my fists, but I felt unseen forces holding down both of my hands. I felt there was something very heavy around my body, and I could not move, even an inch. I fell down on the floor, and I heard you commanding the evil spirts to leave me in Jesus' Name. I felt that spirits left me and I felt very light. Then, you led me to say some prayers to Jesus. You also also asked me to see Father Chua, the pastor of the Blessed Sacrament Parish.

I am happy to inform you that I attended RCIA not long after, and I was baptized as a Roman Catholic a year later. I have been attending the prayer meeting of the Emmaus Charismatic Community on Thursday nights. I also attend Mass almost daily and I pray the Rosary daily in the Carmelite Chapel.

As you also suggested, I have started reading the Bible daily. I am also very active in the Legion of Mary and the St. Joseph Cathedral Chinese Choir.

I feel very close now to the Lord Jesus Christ. Praise and honor to Jesus Christ, my Lord and my Savior!

Valentine Lim
Sarawak, Kuching
Eastern Malaysia

My mother Carolina, who was residing in the Philippines, was diagnosed to have stage 3 colon cancer. My daughter Micah, who was only one year and one month old, was diagnosed with stage 4 liver cancer in March 2012. I was diagnosed with thyroid cancer in June 2012. My daughter went for an intense chemo regimen and several procedures. She also underwent surgeries.

One day, my coworker told me that her grandma had been attending a Mass and Healing Service in St. Luke's Parish in Stockton, and she had been healed of cancer in the Name of Jesus Christ.

We went to Stockton to attend the Mass and Healing Service in April 2013, at the urgings of my coworker. They prayed over me and my daughter. I stood in as proxy for my mom.

Bob Canton, the leader of the group, told me that he discerned that demonic attacks were causing the cancer of the three of us. He told me not to be afraid because Jesus is our Savior and Healer. He asked me to tell my mom to renounce the evil one and to always plead the Blood of Jesus for protection and to go to confession and receive communion daily and to forgive anyone who offended her. He also asked me to do the same. We did what Brother Bob told us to do right away.

We had been coming to St. Luke's not only to attend the Mass and Healing Service monthly but also to attend the prayer meeting weekly, lead by Brother Bob. The members of the prayer group always prayed over me and my daughter, and for my mom in the Philippines, with me as a proxy for her.

In July 2013, three months after we had been attending the Mass and Healing Service and the prayer meeting, the doctors in the Philippines declared my mom free of cancer. Thank God! In August 2013, my doctors in San Francisco told me that all my lab test results are all within normal limits and that I have no more sign of thyroid cancer. We are thanking God every day for these healings. And in June 2014, my daughter was also declared cancer-free.

It has been nine months now that she's been cancer-free! God is the answer! God is good. Jesus rescued us from the evil one. He restored us and healed us! He healed us through the prayers of people from the prayer group. Thank you, Brother Bob, and the healing teams for all the prayers.

God is good. Just believe, surrender everything, and have faith. Don't lose hope.

Brother Bob, thank you for praying for me and my daughter, and for my mom in the Philippines. The healings that we received are truly miracles from God. God bless us all.

Heidi and Ripotola family
Riverbank, California

Prayer to Receive the Gift of Discernment of Spirits

Lord Jesus,
I praise your Holy Name.
Thank you for loving me.
I ask you Lord that your
Holy Spirit will grant me this
spiritual gift of discernment of
spirits for my protection and for the
protection of people around me,
so that I can be an effective
worker for your Kingdom.
Come Holy Spirit and fill me with
your presence and power and
anointing that breaks the yoke.
Come Holy Spirit
and fill me with your love.
I ask this in Jesus' Name, Amen.

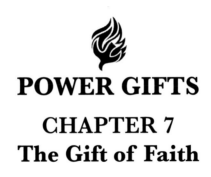

POWER GIFTS
CHAPTER 7
The Gift of Faith

"To one is given through the Spir-
it the expression of faith
by the same Spirit"
—1 Colossians 12:9—

The Charism of Faith—the supernatural
working of the Holy Spirit upon a Christian
that empowers him or her to trust fully that
the Lord will act in a supernatural manner
at a particular time, in a particular situation,
and in a particular place.

The gift of faith inspires a person to pray with God-giv-
en confidence, knowing that what is asked for will be
granted by the Lord. This should not be confused with
the virtue of faith or saving faith. Saving faith is a deep
and passionate belief in the essential facts concerning
the person and work of Jesus Christ. On the other hand,
this "charism" of faith is a kind of faith that can move
mountains. It is a supernatural gift to believe God without doubt.

This charism often operates in association with all the
gifts of the Spirit, most especially the word of knowledge,
healing, miracles, prophecy, and discernment of spirits.

Needless to say, the gift of faith is the necessary ingredient for a Christian to function effectively in the gifts of the Holy Spirit.

One of the great examples of this kind of faith was exhibited by Moses when the Israelites, while being pursued by the Egyptian army, crossed the Red Sea on their way to the Promised Land.

> Then Moses stretched out his hand over the sea; and the Lord drove back the sea with a strong east wind all night long and turned the sea into dry ground. The waters were split, so that the Israelites entered into the midst of the sea on dry land, with the water as a wall to their right and to their left (Exodus 14:21-22).

One dramatic act of this kind of faith in the Old Testament is found in 1 Kings 18:22–39.

> So Elijah said to the people, "I am the only remaining prophet of the LORD, and there are four hundred and fifty prophets of Baal. Give us two young bulls. Let them choose one, cut it into pieces, and place it on the wood, but start no fire. I shall prepare the other and place it on the wood, but shall start no fire. You shall call upon the name of your gods, and I will call upon the name of the Lord. The God who answers with fire is God." All the people answered, "We agree!"

> Elijah then said to the prophets of Baal, "Choose one young bull and prepare it first,

for there are more of you. Call upon your gods, but do not start the fire." Taking the young bull that was turned over to them, they prepared it and called upon Baal from morning to noon, saying, "Baal, answer us!" But there was no sound, and no one answering. And they hopped around the altar they had prepared. When it was noon, Elijah taunted them: "Call louder, for he is a god; he may be busy doing his business, or may be on a journey. Perhaps he is asleep and must be awakened." They called out louder and slashed themselves with swords and spears according to their ritual until blood gushed over them. Noon passed and they remained in a prophetic state until the time for offering sacrifice. But there was no sound, no one answering, no one listening.

Then Elijah said to all the people, "Come here to me." When they drew near to him, he repaired the altar of the LORD which had been destroyed. He took twelve stones, for the number of tribes of the sons of Jacob, to whom the LORD had said: Israel shall be your name. He built the stones into an altar to the name of the LORD, and made a trench around the altar large enough for two measures of grain. When he had arranged the wood, he cut up the young bull and laid it on the wood. He said, "Fill four jars with water and pour it over the burnt offering and over the wood." "Do it again," he said, and they did it again. "Do it a third time," he said, and they did it a third time. The water flowed around the altar; even the trench was filled with the water. At the time for offering sacrifice, Elijah the prophet came forward and said, "LORD, God of Abraham, Isaac, and Israel, let it be known this day that you are God in Israel and that I am your servant and have done all these things at your command. Answer me, LORD! Answer me, that this people may know that you, LORD, are God and that you have turned their hearts back to you." The LORD's fire came down and devoured the burnt offering, wood, stones, and dust, and lapped up the water in the trench. Seeing this, all the people fell prostrate and said, "The LORD is God! The LORD is God!"

Sometime in 2007, I attended a meeting of the Leaders of the Catholic Charismatic Renewal in the United States that was held in Shreveport, Louisiana. On our departure day after the three-day meeting, it was rainy. Consequently, our flight was delayed. A group of us who were already in the airport decided to "bombard" heaven with our prayers, asking the Lord to stop the rain and the stormy weather. Around twenty minutes after we had prayed, the rain stopped, the wind died down, and the sun came out. We were so exhilarated that we started to praise and thank the Lord for answering our prayers.

Father Perry from Alaska and I were on the same flight from Shreveport to Nashville, Tennessee. Our flight was delayed for almost two hours. We had two stops before arriving at our respective final destinations. We had to stop over in Minneapolis/St. Paul from Nashville, before I could proceed to Sacramento, Caifornia, my final destination. Father Perry had to proceed to Seattle from Minneapolis/St. Paul before flying into Juneau, Alaska, the following day.

On our way to Nashville, I asked Father Perry if we could pray together and join our voices in asking the Lord that we be able to catch our flight from Shreveport to Nashville, Tennessee. Otherwise, we would not be able to catch our respective flights going to our final destinations. He asked me to lead the prayer, so I asked the Lord to "please do anything or do something to the airplane, but please do not ground it longer than it is necessary and do not paralyze it. Thank you, Lord, for hearing our prayers."

As soon as we arrived in Nashville, I informed Father Perry that I planned to run so as not to lose much time going to the next terminal where the departure gate of our flight to Minneapolis/St. Paul was situated. Father Perry told me to go ahead. "Bob, I won't discourage you from doing what you plan on doing but I'm afraid it's impossible for us to catch that flight. I believe that flight has already left at least an hour ago," he said. "But I'll try anyway. Who knows? I just sense that the Lord has answered our prayers," was my reply to him. "Go ahead, Bob. I'll just follow you," he replied. So, I went ahead. I was huffing and puffing when I arrived at the gate. I saw some people still milling around the departure area. There was a lady who was wearing a dark-colored, two-piece suit, who looked real worried. So I asked her, "Is this flight going to Nashville, Tennessee?" She answered, "It is supposed to be. But it was just announced that they are still fixing the flat tires of the airplane. It's been over an hour and it is still not being fixed! Can you believe that an airplane has a flat tire? Not only one, but two tires? Give me a break!" She was clearly annoyed and miffed as to what happened to the airplane. I did not have a heart to tell her that we prayed for the Lord to do something to the airplane.

"Father Perry, the angels must be responsible for deflating the tires of the airplane so that it could not leave on time. Otherwise, we would have missed the flight!", I told Father Perry in a joking kind of way, when he arrived at the gate. "You see, the Lord has heard our prayers. Praise His name," I further remarked.

As a result, Father Perry and I arrived at our final destinations on time!

This incident gave me a lesson to trust in the Lord completely. We have to act on our faith.

In James 1:23–25, we read:

> For if anyone is a hearer of the word and not a doer, he is like a man who looks at his own face in a mirror. He sees himself, then goes off and promptly forgets what he looked like. But the one who peers into the perfect law of freedom and perseveres, and is not a hearer who forgets but a doer who acts, such a one shall be blessed in what he does.

Jesus' ministry here on Earth is a demonstration of the awesome power of the Holy Spirit, especially the power of faith.

In John 11:40–42, we read:

> Jesus said to her, "Did I not tell you that if you believe you will see the glory of God?" So they took away the stone. And Jesus raised his eyes

and said, "Father, I thank you for hearing me. I know that you always hear me; but because of the crowd here I have said this, that they may believe that you sent me."

There was woman who had an issue of blood who received her healing because of her tremendous faith in the healing power of Jesus, the Divine Healer. In Mark 5:25–34, we read her story:

> There was a woman afflicted with hemorrhages for twelve years. She had suffered greatly at the hands of many doctors and had spent all that she had. Yet she was not helped but only grew worse. She had heard about Jesus and came up behind him in the crowd and touched his cloak. She said, "If I but touch his clothes, I shall be cured." Immediately her flow of blood dried up. She felt in her body that she was healed of her affliction. Jesus, aware at once that power had gone out from him, turned around in the crowd and asked, "Who has touched my clothes?" But his disciples said to him, "You see how the crowd is pressing upon you, and yet you ask, 'Who touched me?'" And he looked around to see who had done it. The woman, realizing what had happened to her, approached in fear and trembling. She fell down before Jesus and told him the whole truth. He said to her, "Daughter, your faith has saved you. Go in peace and be cured of your affliction."

St. Paul, in the book of Acts, performed a miracle in conjunction with the gift of faith. In Acts 13:6–12, the Word of God says:

> When they had traveled through the whole island as far as Paphos, they met a magician named Bar-Jesus who was a Jewish false prophet. He was with the proconsul Sergius Paulus, a man of intelligence, who had summoned Barnabas and Saul and wanted to hear the word of God. But Elymas the magician (for that is what his name means) opposed them in an attempt to turn the proconsul away from the faith. But Saul, also known as Paul, filled with the holy Spirit, looked intently at him and said, "You son of the devil, you enemy of all that is right, full of every sort of deceit and fraud. Will you not stop twisting the straight paths of [the] Lord? Even now the hand of the Lord is upon you. You will be blind, and unable to see the sun for a time." Immediately a dark mist fell upon him, and he went about seeking people to lead him by the hand. When the proconsul saw what had happened, he came to believe, for he was astonished by the teaching about the Lord.

Indeed, the demonstration of faith and the use of the charism of faith move the heart of God.

Following is one testimony that is a fine example of this charism.

Testimonial
About the Gift of Faith

I had been suffering from rheumatoid arthritis and gout for at least twelve years. Many days the pain in my joints was so severe that I couldn't even get up and walk. It came to a point when I couldn't walk straight without the use of a walker. Before long, I became totally dependent on a walker to walk around.

I learned of the Mass and Healing Service at St. Luke's Parish from reading the Sunday Bulletin of our Church, St. George's, in South Stockton. So, I went to St. Luke's to attend the Mass and Healing Service on a Saturday afternoon.

When I went inside the gym, I saw three people who looked very happy. They were singing hymns while they were setting up the tables and chairs and sound system. I was touched by their warmth and friendliness as they welcomed me with open arms. They let me sit by the door while waiting for all the chairs to be set up. Meanwhile, I noticed that the pain around my knees and feet was gone. A feeling of excitement came all over me. In fact, I walked slowly to the restroom without using my walker even before the Mass and Healing Service had started. (After the service, I learned that during their prayer sessions, the members of the Children of God Prayer Community always ask the Lord Jesus to heal people as soon as they come into the building during the Healing Service.) This is really a great demonstration of faith on their part. After the Mass, the prayer group leader, Bob Canton, announced that the Lord Jesus was healing people who had walking difficulties. I immediately stood up and walked as fast as I could without using the walker, and thank God, without experiencing any pain. I have been walking normally without the use of a walker ever since, and I only have very little pain occasionally around my knees and feet.

I thank the Lord Jesus every day for the healing. I feel like a new person since that day and have been praying and reading the Bible every day.

I submit this testimony to give glory and praise to the Lord Jesus Christ!

Bobbie Fay Cossey
Stockton, California

Robert prayed over this man who was completely blind in his right eye during the prayer meeting at St. Luke's Social Hall in Stockton, California, in October 2018. The man was able to see clearly for the first time in his life.

Prayer to Activate the Charism of Faith

Holy Spirit, the Giver of Faith, I
ask you to grant me the charism of
faith, the kind of faith which Jesus
describes as "the mountain-moving
kind of faith."
I need this kind of faith in order to
be healed, like that of the woman
with the issue of blood.
Lord, above all, use me to give
glory to your Holy Name.
You know, Lord, that this is only
possible if you grant me this gift of
faith to be able to do your works in
your Holy Name.
Thank you, Jesus! Amen.

Robert praying over the sick during the Healing Rally
in El Paso, Texas, in 2013.

POWER GIFTS
CHAPTER 8
The Gift of Healing

Gift of Healing—the gift is the manifestation of the Holy Spirit whereby a physical, psychological, mental, emotional, or spiritual healing, or exorcism or deliverance occurs, which are the results primarily of God's power and action and compassion for His people.

In the Greek of the New Testament, both the words gift and healing are plural.

The Catechism of the Catholic Church asserts that:

Christ's compassion toward the sick and his many healings of every kind of infirmity are a resplendent sign that "God has visited his people"[1] and that the Kingdom of God is close at hand. Jesus has the power not only to heal, but also to forgive sins;[2] he has come to heal the whole man, soul and body; he is the physician the sick have need of"[3] (1503).

In the book, *Prayer for Healing,* under the heading, "Man Confronted by Sickness and Death," page 49, we read:

Christ's meeting with the sick is one of the most human aspects we find in the Gospels. This meeting is for the total, global salvation of the person, and not only to bring bodily health alone, overcome physical sickness and hence avoid "becoming bogged down in the impossible aim of finally defeating death." The meeting between Christ and the sick, is, both in the Gospels and still today, to heal the person in his or her totality, and hence with a dimension of eternity.

According to the *Guidelines on Prayers for Healing*, a booklet published by the Doctrinal Commission of the International Catholic Charismatic Renewal Services (IC-CRS), there are four basic categories of healing, namely physical healing: the healing from physical sickness and disability; psychological healing: the healing of wounds to the human psyche, including emotional wounds; spiritual healing: this means, above all, the "healing from sin" that restores a person to a relationship with God; and exorcism and deliverance. The Catechism of the Catholic Church (1673), states, "Exorcism is directed at the expulsion of demons or to the liberation from demonic possession through spiritual authority which Jesus entrusted to his Church." In contrast, "prayer for deliverance is directed to God, asking God to free someone from the influence of evil spirits," per the *Guidelines on Prayers for Healing*, page 43. Other forms of healing prayer "which require further study, discernment, and pastoral oversight" such as healing of memories, intergenerational healing, and healing of the land," were also mentioned in the book, *Prayer for Healing*.

In my experiences conducting Healing Rallies, Crusades, Retreats, and Workshops, I have perceived that the gift of healing is one of the best tools, if not, the best tool, for evangelization. Many have come to know and believe in the healing, loving, saving power of the Lord Jesus Christ through the ministry of the gift of healing.

In the scriptures are many stories or accounts of God healing the sick, especially in the New Testament. However, only a very few are mentioned in the Old Testament.

In 2 Kings 20:1–6, we read:

> In those days, when Hezekiah was mortally ill, the prophet Isaiah, son of Amoz, came and said to him: "Thus says the LORD: Put your house in order, for you are about to die; you shall not recover." He turned his face to the wall and prayed to the Lord: "Ah, LORD, remember how faithfully and wholeheartedly I conducted myself in your presence, doing what was good in your sight!" And Hezekiah wept bitterly. Before Isaiah had left the central courtyard, the word of the LORD came to him: Go back and tell Hezekiah, the leader of my people: "Thus says the LORD, the God of David your father:
>
> I have heard your prayer;
>   I have seen your tears.
>   Now I am healing you.
> On the third day you shall go up
>   to the house of the LORD.
> I will add to your life fifteen years.
>   I will rescue you and this city

from the hand of the king of Assyria;
  I will be a shield to this city
    for my own sake and the sake of David my servant."

Back in 1997, I led a group of pilgrims to the Holy Land, Egypt, and Jordan. That was my fourth trip to the Holy Land and Egypt and my first to Jordan. While in those countries, I was scheduled to conduct Healing Services at the holy sites we visited.

After visiting the Church of the Nativity in Bethlehem, we went to Mariam Coptic Church, which is about three blocks away from the Church of the Nativity, to conduct a Healing Service.

Our group was met by the priest, Father Yacob, at the entrance of the church, and he introduced himself to our group. "Brother Canton, so you are here to pray for healing?" I said, "Yes, Father Yacob." He said, "You know, in my church there are many sick people." "Yes, I see them," I replied back to him. The church was packed with mostly Palestinian Christians, according to him. "You know, Brother Canton, I have a very close friend who needs healing badly," he further told me. I told him that "we are here to pray for everyone who needs healing."

After our group sang a few praise and worship songs, I started to preach the Word of God, with Father Yacob as my interpreter. Afterwards, Father Yacob took a man by the hand from the entrance of the church to the altar. He told me, "Brother Canton, this is George Habab, a friend of mine. You know how many years he has been blind?" I told him, "I do not have any idea." He said, "he has been blind since birth. He is 58 years old."

I looked at George. I could only see the "whites in his eyes." I could not even see his pupils in both eyes.

"Brother Canton, he is yours," and then Father Yacob walked away, stayed by the altar, and folded his arms, with a half smile on his face. I believe, he probably said to himself, "let's see what he can do for George."

I said a prayer to the Holy Spirit in Jesus' Name. In short, my prayer was like this, "Help Lord! I need you, Lord, please help! This is a hard case, as you know, but nothing is impossible for you. I know this is very easy for you."

I asked the congregation to extend their hands towards George. In the silence of my heart, I said this to the Lord, "Lord, you were born not far away from here. You probably played on this very holy ground in your younger days. Lord Jesus, you are the Master Healer, and your reputation is at stake." The Lord spoke into my heart, saying, "Trust me, my son, and do not be anxious about anything." As I laid hands on this man's eyes, I commanded the blindness to go in Jesus' mighty Name and I asked the Holy Spirit to open George's eyes. I asked Him to do creative miracles such as brand new pupils, brand new cornea, brand new optic nerves, brand new iris, and brand new eyes. Minutes later, George was saying, I can see some shadows. I asked the congregation to keep on praying for him. Then he said, "I can see some light." I kept on praising and thanking the Holy Trinity for this miracle. Minutes later, George said, "I can see your face, I can see your nose, your eyes, your entire face, I can see what you are wearing." I asked him, "Do you like what you see?" in a joking kind of way. George did not give me an answer. So, "I believe George decided to remain silent rather than to tell the truth," I declared, to the laughter of the congregation.

Then I asked George to test his vision, to follow what I would be doing with both my hands and arms, while keeping a distance of around seven feet from him. George was able to imitate everything I did with my hands. Glory be to God! George was crying and sobbing uncontrollably, thanking and praising God. I told George that the Lord was telling him in my heart, "My son, I heard your prayers. I want you to continue to follow me for I have great plans for you. I want you to tell every person that you meet that I, your Lord and God, am a loving God. I love you, my son."

Later on, the Palestinian women ran towards where I was, and I was startled. They were fighting over my hands, and they put my hands wherever they wanted to put them on themselves. I asked Father Yacob to stop them from doing what they were doing, otherwise we would leave. I told the women that I didn't want anyone to get hurt. I, for one, almost fell down. I reminded them that I'm not a healer, but Jesus is. I'm only a mere instrument of His healing touch. I could not heal even a lowly fly. I also exhorted them that they should focus their hearts and minds and their whole beings to the Lord Jesus Christ because He is the source of life, and every good thing comes from Him.

Many healings took place in that Church after we prayed with them. Praise Jesus, the Divine Healer!

Over a year later, I led another pilgrimage to the Holy Land and in Italy.

While most of the pilgrims in our group were in the Church of the Nativity, I asked three people in our group to accompany me to Mariam Church to visit Father Yacob and to inquire about George Habab.

When I saw the priest, we exchanged pleasantries and, thank God, he still remembered me. I asked him about George. "Oh, George, you could seldom see him here anymore," he informed me with a sad face. I thought something bad had happened to him. I asked him why. "Oh, he has been out there sight-seeing," Father Yacob informed me.

Really, I could not blame George.

In retrospect, I can see how five different charisms — the word of knowledge, the word of wisdom, healings, miracles, and prophecy had been manifested or at interplay on that occasion through the power of the Holy Spirit.

In the Gospels, we read many accounts of Jesus healing the sick. In fact, more than seventy percent of Jesus' ministry here on earth was spent on healing the sick and the frail. Every person who came to Jesus for healing, He healed. He is a God full of compassion and love for His people.

The Word of God says in Matthew 9:35–37:

> Jesus went around to all the towns and villages, teaching in their synagogues, proclaiming the gospel of the kingdom, and curing every disease and illness. At the sight of the crowds, his heart was moved with pity for them because they were troubled and abandoned, like sheep without a shepherd. Then he said to his disciples, "The harvest is abundant but the laborers are few; so ask the master of the harvest to send out laborers for his harvest."

In Matthew 8:1–4, we read:

> When Jesus came down from the mountain, great crowds followed him. And then a leper approached, did him homage, and said,

113

"Lord, if you wish, you can make me clean." He stretched out his hand, touched him, and said, "I will do it. Be made clean." His leprosy was cleansed immediately. Then Jesus said to him, "See that you tell no one, but go show yourself to the priest, and offer the gift that Moses prescribed; that will be proof for them."

In Matthew 9:1–8, the Word of God says:

He entered a boat, made the crossing, and came into his own town. And there people brought to him a paralytic lying on a stretcher. When Jesus saw their faith, he said to the paralytic, "Courage, child, your sins are forgiven." At that, some of the scribes said to themselves, "This man is blaspheming." Jesus knew what they were thinking, and said, "Why do you harbor evil thoughts? Which is easier, to say, 'Your sins are forgiven,' or to say, 'Rise and walk'? But that you may know that the Son of Man has authority on earth to forgive sins"—he then said to the paralytic, "Rise, pick up your stretcher, and go home." He rose and went home. When the crowds saw this they were struck with awe and glorified God who had given such authority to human beings.

Also, in Matthew 9:27–31, we read:

And as Jesus passed on from there, two blind men followed [him], crying out, "Son of David, have pity on us!" When he entered the house, the blind men approached him and Jesus said to them, "Do you believe that I can do this?" "Yes, Lord," they said to him. Then he touched their eyes and said, "Let it be done for you according to your faith." And their eyes were opened. Jesus warned them sternly, "See that no one knows about this." But they went out and spread word of him through all that land.

Jesus also sets those who are captives, free from the clutches of Satan. In Matthew 8:28–34, the Word of God says:

> When he came to the other side, to the territory of the Gadarenes, two demoniacs who were coming from the tombs met him. They were so savage that no one could travel by that road. They cried out, "What have you to do with us, Son of God? Have you come here to torment us before the appointed time?" Some distance away a herd of many swine was feeding. The demons pleaded with him, "If you drive us out, send us into the herd of swine." And he said to them, "Go then!" They came out and entered the swine, and the whole herd rushed down the steep bank into the sea where they drowned. The swineherds ran away, and when they came to the town they reported everything, including what had happened to the demoniacs. Thereupon the whole town came out to meet Jesus,

and when they saw him they begged him to leave their district.

These are just a few of the healings that Jesus did while He was still walking on the face of the earth. In John 21:25, St. John says:

> There are also many other things that Jesus did, but if these were to be described individually, I do not think the whole world would contain the books that would be written.

I would like to share some of the healing testimonies that I have received over the years in my capacity as God's instrument or vessel in healing the sick.

Testimonials
About the Gift of Healing

Dear Bob,

I received some testimonies from Okinawa.

Sister Johanna's deafness was healed instantly and now she feels it's too noisy and needs some adjustment by God. She does not use her hearing aids anymore and she had lost them! Her eyes were healed at the same time. She used to wear glasses, but after you prayed over her for healing, she could see clearly again. If she uses glasses, she is unable to see. But, as she drives every day, and her driving license is with the glasses on, there was no other choice but to wear glasses while driving. She is going to the doctor to ask him what to do now.

There was a person who had something in her throat, and she was unable to look downward without any irritation and pain. She was planning to get it checked at the hospital. But, instead, she came to the Kanto Conference in Chiba, unexpectedly. She came with great determination to get healed. When you asked those attending to place their hands to their foreheads or to any parts of their bodies that were hurting or needed healing, she put her hands on her throat while you were praying for healing for everybody.

After the prayers, she had no more pain when she bent her head. She said she felt something came out from her throat while you were praying, commanding sickness to leave in the name of Jesus.

A lady was told by her doctor that her bleeding was not curable and she had to live with it. But she was healed completely when you prayed over her. There is no more bleeding. She told me she was going to tell her Buddhist doctor that Jesus healed her.

There were many more healings, but as I do not know the details, I cannot mention them now. Bob, by the way, can you stop over in Tokyo next year for a few days of ministering here on your way to Okinawa? People have been inquiring when you are coming back to Tokyo again. Please inform me of your coming.

With our warmest wishes and prayers,
Kaoru Masuda
Tokyo, Japan

Dear Mr. Canton,
Last year during your Healing Workshop here in St. Francis of Assisi Church in Las Vegas, I asked you to pray for the healings of my breast cancer and the disability of my spine and other ailments.

A month and a half after you prayed over me, in November 2012, I went to my oncologist for checkups. He ordered an MRI, scan, and other tests for me. After all the test results came in, the doctor told me, "I have great news for you. The cancer is no longer present in your body." Yes, I've been cancer free. My spine was also healed, and I don't have any more back pain. My blood pressure has also been normal. My doctors ordered me not to take any more high blood pressure medications.

Thank you very much for your prayers for me. I am so happy, and I've been telling my relatives and friends what happened to me after the Healing Workshop. I thank God every day, and I've been praying for you and your ministry. May He always bless you and your good work and your ministry.

Sincerely,
Lulu J. Dimain
Henderson,NV.

Hello Brother Bob:

My name is Bernadette and I met you at Church of the Ascension, Elmhurst, Queens, New York, November 2018. I had brought two friends with me to attend the Miracle and Healing Rally. One of them was an eighty-six-year-old lady named Gizzele, who had arthritis in her knees. You prayed over her during the Healing and Miracle Rally that you conducted. A few days went by and still she had no relief. As we were coming down the chapel steps at the St.Bartholomew Church in Elmhurst ,Queens, two to three days later, she seemed so excited. She said, "Bernadette, guess what?" My knees are healed. I realized it when I was climbing the stairs, going downstairs, and walking. She was so excited that she said she felt like dancing. Her arthritis is gone! Healed! She had been suffering from arthritis for many, many years. As you have proclaimed Brother Bob, "Jesus is the Healer!"

My other friend named Paulette had also received a healing from Jesus through your prayers. She said you prayed over her and you commanded her large thyroid tumor in the right side of her throat to leave in the Name of Jesus. She gave her testimony that same night during the prayer meeting that the mass or tumor had disappeared without a trace. Praise you Jesus!

Bernadette Penny
Queens, New York

Brother Bob,

Praise the Lord for his mercy through you, that I witnessd many healings during the Retreat and Healing Seminar sponsored by the Filipino Catholic Charismatic Communities in Rome.

Recently, I talked with some people who attended the Healing Rally. One person had eye problems because of diabetes, and he received his healing; a teenager with a blind eye that consequently affected the other eye, now can see again; some tumors gone; many deaf people were able to hear; many suffering from back pains were healed; and healings of rheumatism, asthma, and allergies took place, including inner healing and many more. God showed up and many were touched. We are waiting for you to come back in June to Assisi for the ICCRS Conference and also for your return here in Rome and in Milan this coming September for a series of workshops and Healing Rallies.

Thank you Brother Bob for sharing with us the Grace of God, and the joy in your heart and your humility was felt by those around you..

GOD IS REALLY ALIVE and moving through you! And HE LOVES US ALL! I also informed Oreste and Amelia in the ICCRS office about God's favor for us here during your visit.

Keeping you and your family in our prayers.

GOD BLESS YOU!

Judy Maramot
Rome, Italy

Dear Robert Canton,

It was the August 25, 2018, when I attended the Annual Grand Assembly of the Filipino Canadian Catholic Charismatic Prayer Communities (FCCCPC). I had an aircast on my left foot. I had been walking and with a limp as a result of a fractured ankle. The pain was really excruciating.

My purpose in attending this event was to listen to the guest speakers, to learn, to be inspired, to go home with a flaming heart, and a zeal to serve the Lord.

I had heard that one of the guest speakers was from California named Robert Canton, who is an instrument in healing many people with different illnesses. Since I had a foot fracture, I told myself to give it a try to be prayed over but did not expect anything. Towards the mid-morning while listening, I had an unusual feeling. My heart was beating fast and I was nervous as if something unusual would happen, not knowing where this was coming from. This feeling of nervousness did not even lead me to think that the Holy Spirit was giving me a message; that something great would take place, and that it was being revealed to me.

After the Mass, the talk of Robert Canton on healing followed. After his talk, Robert started calling out the healings that he said the Lord was doing among the attendees. Again, I felt nervous and my heart was beating faster and faster. I was seated way back in the last seat in the auditorium. Brother Robert spotted me and called me to come forward. He asked me to stand at the middle aisle, and I waited for him. I was surprised and I was thinking "why me?" He asked me if I wanted to be healed, and my answer was yes. I knew that anyone who had some sort of illness or injury would never say no, and would want very much to be free from pain and suffering. While he was praying for me, using the Name and the precious blood of Jesus, I also started to pray, surrendering myself and believing that Jesus is the true healer using Brother Robert as His instrument. He asked me to take off my aircast and to try walking around the auditorium. I was able to walk but still with a bit of pain. Brother Robert continued to pray until I could walk normally without any pain whatsoever. Then I started running inside the auditorium. I could see people jumping up and down, some crying, some clapping their hands and praising God. I had tears in my eyes; tears of happiness, tears of a grateful heart.

The following day, I went to see my doctor who ordered a scan and MRI for me. The results that the doctor relayed to me were unbelievable. He said the results show a competely healed fracture, and the bones were fused together as if no fracture had ever occurred in my left foot.

Jesus is really awesome!

With this beautiful experience, it gave me an affirmation to continue serving the Lord and be His instrument.

Thank you Brother Robert Canton. You will always be in my prayers for your ministry and your family. I hope and pray that you would come back to Toronto soon. Many are waiting for your return.

Gratefully yours,
Marybel Jose
Toronto, Canada

Wow! What a very powerful weekend! I received much! What a blessing Robert (Bob) Canton is; such a humble, obedient, gifted, humorous, full of the Spirit, man of God! I purchased his book at the conference, *Miracles Never Ending,* and have had a hard time putting it down, as he shares his powerful testimony and countless others, as well as teachings and prayers that are faith-lifting and encouraging! Three prayers are included in the back of the book that he recommends to be prayed every day! I highly recommend that you purchase a copy of his book–it is a must-have! You will not be disappointed (Amazon.com)! I have been printing off copies of the three prayers Bob recommended and am sharing with those who are sick. The entire book will bless you!

Helen Kelly
Saint John
Sackville, New Brunswick, Canada

It was with great anticipation for the conference of 2016, to meet and witness Bob Canton and his gift of healing ministry. I got to witness first-hand Our Lord Jesus Christ at work. Before it started on Friday night, we the prayer teams, word ministry, and music ministry met with Bob for direction and prayer. Bob had asked the prayer partners to disperse throughout the hall to be ready for those who would need assistance or direction where Bob was concerned. When he came out after introduction and prayer, he immediately received a word of knowledge. He stated there was someone who had poor knees and found it hard to stand. A lady in my row put her hand up right away. I could see she was having great difficulty standing. My prayer partner, at that time, had gone to the washroom, so I asked her sister to assist me in getting this lady down front to Bob. She was having great difficulty walking. Bob prayed over her with a crucifix in his hand then told us to let her go. She was very fearful at first, but she stood on her own. Then Bob beckoned for her to walk towards him. She protested but, with his coaxing, she took a few shaky steps, and with his faith in her ability to walk, she started walking without limping and straightened up. He then asked her to skip or jump. She protested again, but then she did it. It was miraculous in that I know she could hardly stand upon going down front, and she really leaned on us to get there. I saw her throughout the weekend and she walked without a limp or being hunched over. I am so blessed to have been part of such a healing through the living Christ. Praise His Holy Name.

Joyce White,
Charlottetown, PEI

At the Atlantic Conference on Saturday, it was a day that was very powerful for me. Since 2009, I was wearing hearing aids in both ears. God healed my hearing in both ears after Bob Canton commanded the deafness to go in Jesus' Name. I no longer need hearing aids. I am very thankful to God. I praise Him for his kindness and mercy. Honor to your Name Lord Jesus Christ! Alleluia!

Mary Martin,
Saint John, NB, Canada

Dear Bob:

Thank you so much for your awesome book, *Miracles Never Ending*. I had ordered the book from Amazon.com upon the recommendation of dear Fe Enriquez and I was not disappointed. Not only did it tie scripture and teaching points together, it was amazing to read the many personal testimonies of people who were healed in the Name of Jesus, through your fervent prayers, gift of knowledge, and prophecy. It was also humorous at times, but most of all it gave me many times to pause, reflect, praise and thank God's almighty power, ongoing healing, and love for His children.

I like that you have quoted multiple scriptures to a given topic, which gives emphasis to Jesus' teachings. I like that you've included the powerful prayers that could affect a change for healing and that you've outlined the steps we need to know to pray effectively. The various testimonies are what strengthens the teachings in your book. These are what makes a difference from other books. I have not seen so many testimonies from people from other countries collected in a single book that I've read on prayers for healing. Thank you, Bob, for sharing your knowledge and gifts from the Holy Spirit! I will recommend this book to my family and friends, because I know many of them are in need of healing due to multiple medical problems.

I knew while reading your book, I was already planning to find out how we could attend your next healing service, but when I came to the personal testimony regarding spinal stenosis on page 182 of your book, it gave us much hope and we knew it was the answer to our prayers for how we were going to deal with Blit's spinal stenosis of C4-C7 and bone spur. So, I left my dear friend, Fe, a message to find out when your next healing service was. Because she was genuinely concerned and wanted to help, she immediately contacted you and informed us that you were willing to pray over Blit via phone because of his constant pain, rather than wait until we go see you at the next Healing Service that you would conduct.

We are so grateful to you for returning our call and taking the time to pray over Blit for his constant pain and numbness due to spinal stenosis. Thank God, his back pain and numbness have disappeared after you prayed over him. It was so amazing, and we cannot thank God enough. God is really good. We also thank dear Fe for facilitating this call and for her prayers as well. It was amazing how you pray for someone who is sick. You were full of compassion and gentleness and empathy for the sick. I will pray daily the Healing and Keeping Prayer in the back of your book.

We give praise, honor, and glory to God Our Father and Jesus our Lord, and we thank you, Bob, for your graciousness and zeal in being an instrument of God's healing love. We pray for your ministry's continued success and will keep you and your family in our prayers. We thank you from the bottom of our hearts.

We hope to see you in Stockton for your next Healing and Prayer Service.

With love and gratitude,
Elena and Blit Angeles
San Francisco, California

Hi Bro. Bob Canton,
Praise and thanks to God, for He is the Great Healer!

On Pentecost weekend, May 23-25, 2015, you were in the Catholic Chinese Church, Edmonton, Alberta, Canada. God healed many people from illnesses through you. I was one of them. I got healed from hearing loss. I attended the second day of your crusade, May 24, to be exact. I volunteered to be one of the choir members, and when you called those people with hearing problems to come in front of the altar, I came to be prayed over by you. When you prayed over me, I felt like there was a strong but gentle wind that had enveloped my entire body. I went down on the floor, an experience which you described as, "resting in the Spirit." I experienced total peace while on the floor of the church.

Later on, when I got up from the floor, I was amazed that I could hear everything that you said without my hearing aids. GOD HEALED ME RIGHT THERE!!! PRAISE and thank you, JESUS. I was one of those eight people who received healing of deafness. I thank God also for using you as His instrument to heal people. Since then, I have not worn my hearing aids again. I had been wearing my hearing aids for seven years, but not anymore. As you said, everything is possible for God. My family is also amazed by what happened to me, and I have started praying on a regular basis and reading the Bible as you advised and receiving the Eucharist on a regular basis.

I have been praying for you and your family for God to bless, protect, and use you whenever and wherever He leads you. In Jesus' name. Amen.

Sincerely,
Daisy Dable Gogerla
Edmonton, Canada

My father Gilberto Lopez was hard of hearing. He'd been having issues for a few years now and had gone to the doctor and was referred to an ear specialist to get his ear checked, but they couldn't find anything wrong with him. However, he was losing his hearing each day and it was getting worse. I am a witness to this, as I would have to be pretty loud when carrying on a conversation with him.

My mother indicated she had to yell at him, and even then he still had problems hearing her. During the healing service on Friday, October 7, 2016, at St. James Church in McMinnville, Oregon, brother Bob Canton prayed over him, and he was healed from his hearing problem. He is now able to hear clearly in both ears. Now we don't have to yell at him anymore. Thank you Lord!

A lady named Elodia couldn't sleep, and she had been taking medication for the depression and, in spite of the medications, she still had that depression.

During that same healing service at St. James Church on Friday, October 7, Elodia was healed from the depression. She had been battling with this for years. She said that during the Healing Rally when Bob Canton prayed over her, she felt that something came out of her, and the depression left her. She told me days after the rally that ever since then, she has been able to sleep well as never before. She praises the Lord for the healing that she received that weekend. She indicated the Lord is so good to us. Glory be to God!

Irene Flores
McMinville, Oregon

Brother Bob,

Thank you for your recent mission at St. James, Okotoks, Canada (Diocese of Calgary). There were many people who reported many healings to me. It was great for you to come on Pentecost weekend. Your teachings and your ministry were excellent. I'm sure my parish will never be the same again. I was happy to see that the gym, which holds 270, was in full capacity, in fact, it was standing room only, but at the same time sad that we had to turn people away for lack of space. I hope to see you again in the near future. I offered the Mass for you and your brother Nilo and with your families.

May God bless you!
Fr. Yarek SDS
Okotoks, Canada

Prayer to Receive the Charism of Healing

Lord Jesus, in your Words you said,
"The works that I do, you will do
also, and greater works shall you do
because I go to the Father." I ask
you now that your Holy Spirit,
the Giver of gifts, the Advocate,
will endow me with the gift of healings, so that I can be an effective
instrument to heal the sick and to
spread the Good News that you are
the Master Healer and that you are
still healing your people, for your
greater glory and honor.
I ask this in your mighty Name,
oh Lord Jesus, Amen

Chapter 8 Endnotes

1. Lk 7:16; cf. Mt 4:24.
2. Cf. Mk 2:5-12.
3. Cf. Mk 2:17.

POWER GIFTS
CHAPTER 9
The Gift of Miracles
and Working of Miracles

*"To one is given through
the Spirit... mighty deeds;..."*
—1 Corinthians 12:8, 10—

The Gift of Miracles—Miracles are the so-called events that violate the laws of nature. The Gift of Miracles is a God-given ability to demonstrate the supernatural power of the Holy Spirit at work. This power is described in the Greek word as "dunamis," meaning "dynamite" or "power."

Jesus is a miracle worker par excellence because He was led by the Holy Spirit, guided by the Holy Spirit, controlled by the Holy Spirit, filled with the Holy Spirit, and empowered by the Holy Spirit. Jesus' apostles and disciples such as Peter, Paul, Philip, and others, also were used by the Holy Spirit to do the miraculous.

The Charism of Miracles is one of the best and the most effective weapons of our warfare and one of the best tools for evangelization.

If many Christians would take the Words of the Son of God to heart and act on them, this world would never be the same.

> Amen, amen, I say to you, whoever believes in me will do the works that I do, and will do greater ones than these, because I am going to the Father. And whatever you ask in my name, I will do, so that the Father may be glorified in the Son. If you ask anything of me in my name, I will do it (John 14:12-14).

The same Holy Spirit who empowered Jesus to do what He did while He was still walking on this earth is with us and upon us. The same power that raised Jesus from the dead is within us.

It is the most exciting time to be alive in this day and age, because the Holy Spirit is very active in the world today.

I, for one, have seen and witnessed signs and wonders and miracles beyond description because our God is limitless. Glory to His Holy Name!

In 1 Corinthians 2:9–10, St. Paul says:

> ..."What eye has not seen, and ear has
>   not heard,
>   and what has not entered the
>   human heart,
>   what God has prepared for those
>   who love him,"

this God has revealed to us through the Spirit.

> For the Spirit scrutinizes everything, even the
> depths of God.

Jesus' first instructions to His disciples had been "As you go, make this proclamation: "The kingdom of heaven is at hand. Cure the sick, raise the dead, cleanse lepers, drive out demons" (Matthew 10:7–8).

One time, John the Baptist sent his disciples to ask Jesus:

> "Are you who is to come or should we look
> for another?" Jesus said to them in re-
> ply: "Go and tell John what you hear and
> see: the blind regain their sight, the lame
> walk, lepers are cleansed, the deaf hear,
> the dead are raised, and the poor have the
> good news proclaimed to them. And bless-
> ed is the one who takes no offense at me"
> (Matthew 11:3–6).

Jesus also states in Acts 1:8:

> But you will receive power when the holy
> Spirit comes upon you, and you will be my
> witnesses in Jerusalem, throughout Judea and
> Samaria, and to the ends of the earth.

The Lord is always true to His promises.

In the Catholic Charismatic Renewal, the Lord has raised up many men and women, members of the clergy, the religious, and lay people, who have very active ministries of healing and miracles.

Today it is very common to hear from people, even Christians, that the age of miracles was only true and active during the time of Jesus. However, it is very true in this day and age. Miracles do still happen, although the number of Christians who believe that the Lord can and may use them to do miracles in His Name is far less in number today.

In Hebrews 13:8, we read: "Jesus Christ is the same yesterday, today, and forever." The same Jesus who did all kinds of miracles while He was still walking is still doing them now by the power of the Holy Spirit.

The ministry of Jesus is geared towards the establishment of God's Kingdom. The Kingdom of God ended the dominion of Satan over the world, which was present since the fall of our first parents, Adam and Eve.

In Matthew 12:28, Jesus says: "But if it is by the Spirit of God that I drive out demons, then the kingdom of God has come upon you."

> Then they came to Capernaum, and on the sabbath he entered the synagogue and taught. The people were astonished at his teaching, for he taught them as one having authority and not as the scribes. In their synagogue was a man with an unclean spirit; he cried out, "What have you to do with us, Jesus of Nazareth? Have you come to destroy us? I know who you are—the Holy One of God!" Jesus rebuked him and said, "Quiet! Come out of him!" The unclean spirit convulsed him and with a loud cry came out of him. All were amazed and asked one another, "What is this? A new teaching with authority. He commands even the unclean spirits and they obey him." His fame spread everywhere throughout the whole region of Galilee (Mark 1:21–28).

I vividly remember the time when I ministered in St. Edward's Church in Newark, California, around thirty-five miles south of San Francisco. As I was about to pray over a woman, I noticed that she was looking at me "with piercing eyes and a very angry look on her face." I discerned right way that there were some evil spirits in her. As soon as I laid hands on her, I asked Jesus to cover me and those who were present including the woman, and the "catcher" behind her with the precious blood of Jesus in faith.

This woman let out a loud shriek as she fell down on the floor after I laid hands on her. As soon as her body hit the floor, she started to spin around like a blade of a helicopter, screaming at the top of her voice, "I hate you, I hate you," numerous times. Some people had run away in fright.

As she was spinning around, she got a hold of the hem of my pants, and I almost fell down. She exhibited extraordinary strength. Four people had to hold her down, but she almost got away.

I kept on rebuking the spirits of hatred, anger, rebellion, divination, and spirits of occultism in the mighty name of Jesus through the intercession of Mary and St. Joseph. Somebody took some holy water and sprinkled it on her. She screamed, "it hurts, it hurts." I placed a crucifix on her forehead while I continued to rebuke the spirits tormenting her to leave by the Blood of Jesus through the power of the Holy Spirit. She finally calmed down, and then I led her to renounce the evil spirits in Jesus' name and to invite Jesus to come and be the Lord and Savior of her life. I also was able to pray with her for "inner healing" in Jesus' Name. That evening, she was also able to avail herself of the Sacraments of Reconciliation and the

Eucharist, which are the best sources of healing, glory be to God!

I was just thankful that I did not lose my pants. That alone was a "miracle." I really held on to them with all my might. As this woman got a hold of my pants and tried to pull me down with all her might, I kept on adjuring the spirits in her to stop in Jesus' Name and by His precious Blood. I said to myself, *Lord, please let your ministering angels assist me so that I will not lose my pants, otherwise my wife will not let me into the house.* Really, it was a very close call for me. I would have been out in the cold without my pants had she succeeded.

In Deuteronomy 31:8, the Word of God says:

> It is the LORD who goes before you; he will
> be with you and will never fail you or forsake
> you. So do not fear or be dismayed.

In Mark 8:1–9, we read about Jesus multiplying seven loaves of bread and a few fish to feed 4,000 hungry people.

> In those days when there again was a great
> crowd without anything to eat, he summoned
> the disciples and said, "My heart is moved
> with pity for the crowd, because they have
> been with me now for three days and have
> nothing to eat. If I send them away hungry
> to their homes, they will collapse on the way,
> and some of them have come a great dis-
> tance." His disciples answered him, "Where
> can anyone get enough bread to satisfy them
> here in this deserted place?" Still he asked
> them, "How many loaves do you have?"

THE GIFT OF MIRACLES AND WORKING OF MIRACLES

"Seven," they replied. He ordered the crowd to sit down on the ground. Then, taking the seven loaves he gave thanks, broke them, and gave them to his disciples to distribute, and they distributed them to the crowd. They also had a few fish. He said the blessing over them and ordered them distributed also. They ate and were satisfied. They picked up the fragments left over—seven baskets. There were about four thousand people.

In Matthew 20:29–34, the Word of God says:

As they left Jericho, a great crowd followed him. Two blind men were sitting by the roadside, and when they heard that Jesus was passing by, they cried out, "Son of David, have pity on us!" The crowd warned them to be silent, but they called out all the more, "Lord, Son of David, have pity on us!" Jesus stopped and called them and said, "What do you want me to do for you?" They answered him, "Lord, let our eyes be opened." Moved with pity, Jesus touched their eyes. Immediately they received their sight, and followed him.

And in Mark 7:31–37 it reads:

Again he left the district of Tyre and went by way of Sidon to the Sea of Galilee, into the district of the Decapolis. And people brought to him a deaf man who had a speech impediment and begged him to lay his hand on him.

He took him off by himself away from the crowd. He put his finger into the man's ears and, spitting, touched his tongue; then he looked up to heaven and groaned, and said to him, *"Ephphatha!"* (that is, "Be opened!") And [immediately] the man's ears were opened, his speech impediment was removed, and he spoke plainly. He ordered them not to tell anyone. But the more he ordered them not to, the more they proclaimed it. They were exceedingly astonished and they said, "He has done all things well. He makes the deaf hear and [the] mute speak."

Sometime in the late summer of 1999, a group of us from the Children of God Prayer Community in St. Luke's Parish in Stockton, California, was asked by the Catholic Chaplain, Father Paul Manzano, to conduct a Life in the Spirit Seminar in the Northern California Women's Prison in Stockton.

As I was about to conclude my talk on "Salvation," the Holy Spirit prompted me to call out a Word of Knowledge that He gave. The Lord said, "I'm healing a woman prisoner here who has been deaf for a long time." I was startled when I received this message from the Lord. So, I spoke this message out to the prisoners. Nobody said anything. So I spoke it again. Suddenly a woman with tattoos on her arms was jumping up and down, crying and praising God at the same time. She said, "I can hear, I can hear, oh my God, I can hear!"

The rest of the prisoners joined her in praising God. So I called her up to the front of the hall to relate to us what happened to her. She said that her name was Sandra and she belonged to a Hopi Native American tribe in Northern California. She further said someone had shot her a long time ago and the bullet had pierced her eardrum. Since that time, she had been deaf. She could only communicate with sign language. So I asked her to turn her back to me, and I stood about four feet away from her. I asked her to repeat every word that I would say to her to test her hearing. She repeated everything I said to her with clarity. Everybody was shouting and praising God, including my companions!

The Lord, no doubt, was glorified through the healing of this woman. Indeed this is one miracle that I will never forget in my life because I believe it had impacted the lives of those women prisoners.

The entire facility heard about what had happened. During the Healing Service that evening in the Chapel, many were turned away because it was "standing room only." The prison guards were also there in full force, and they heard and witnessed many more healings in Jesus' Name! Praise Jesus, the Miracle Worker!

One of the greatest miracles that Jesus did was the raising of the widow's son at Nain. In Luke 7:11–17, we read:

> Soon afterward he journeyed to a city called Nain, and his disciples and a large crowd accompanied him. As he drew near to the gate of the city, a man who had died was being carried out, the only son of his mother, and she was a widow. A large crowd from the city was with her. When the Lord saw her, he was moved with pity for her and said to her, "Do not weep." He stepped forward and touched the coffin; at this

the bearers halted, and he said, "Young man, I tell you, arise!" The dead man sat up and began to speak, and Jesus gave him to his mother. Fear seized them all, and they glorified God, exclaiming, "A great prophet has arisen in our midst," and "God has visited his people." This report about him spread through the whole of Judea and in all the surrounding region.

I believe that Jesus' greatest miracle was His own resurrection as related in Matthew 28, Mark 16, Luke 24, and John 20.

Every opportunity that I have when giving the teachings on "How to Receive and Use the Power of God," I always emphasize that Christians should not follow signs and wonders and miracles and healings. Signs and wonders and miracles and healings should follow Christians wherever they are and wherever they go.

In Mark 16:17–18, Jesus says:

> These signs will accompany those who believe: in my name they will drive out demons, they will speak new languages. They will pick up serpents [with their hands], and if they drink any deadly thing, it will not harm them. They will lay hands on the sick, and they will recover.

Every baptized Christian is imbued with the power from the Holy Spirit, not just bishops or priests or the religious, or a few chosen ones. Every Christian has the opportunity and the power at his disposal to turn this darkened world upside down and inside out for God's glory through the power of the Holy Spirit.

In Acts 1:8, Jesus says:

> But you will receive power when the holy
> Spirit comes upon you, and you will be my
> witnesses in Jerusalem, throughout Judea and
> Samaria, and to the ends of the earth.

I could never forget an experience I had when I went to Pontiac, Michigan, a suburb of Detroit, back in 2011. After I conducted a Healing Crusade in St. Damien of Molokai Church, a lady came up to me to plead with me earnestly to go to Harper University Hospital with her because her husband had been comatose for more than two months. She said, "Frank has suffered a massive stroke, and we have just decided to take him off the life support system. Please come with me to the hospital so that you can pray for him for whatever the Lord's will is for his life. My family members are really distraught about Frank's condition." I felt really sorry for the lady, so I decided to go with her.

In Frank's hospital room, it seemed like he was not moving at all. I could not even tell whether he was breathing. So, I made a sign of the Cross on his forehead and started praying over him. I commanded his brain to function normally, in Jesus' Name, as well as his limbic system, lobes, brain stem, and cerebellum. In Jesus' Name, I also commanded his primary motor cortex, his motor system, and motor cells to function normally, and his paralysis to be healed completely. Then I heard the Lord speak into my heart. He said, "Speak life into his body, my son, in my name and through the power of the Holy Spirit, and you will see amazing results." Thereafter, I obeyed what the Lord was telling me in my heart. Then, I felt a tap on my back. When I looked back, it was Frank's wife. She told me, "Bob, ask the Lord for a quick and happy death for him." I was flummoxed. Then I thought to myself, *the Lord has just asked me to speak life into him. I better obey the Lord's commands no matter what and just ignore her.* So, I said two more times, "In Jesus' Name, I speak life into Frank and through the power of the Holy Spirit." Frank's wife had tapped my back three more times, saying, "Bob, please pray for a quick and happy death for him," but I just ignored her. When I was done praying over Frank, I explained to his wife that I had to obey the promptings and commands of the Lord.

Six hours later, Frank had awakened from the coma. After three weeks, he was released from the hospital.

More than two years later, I was back in Pontiac, Michigan. When I was on the steps of the entrance of the Church, a man came to meet me and gave me a bear hug. He asked, "Do you remember me, Bob? I'm Frank. They told me that you prayed over me in the hospital more than two years ago. I am now a member of a prayer group here in Pontiac, and I am a member of the Hospitality Committee. I'm going to take care of you real good this weekend." I hardly recognized him because he was full of energy and life! Praise Jesus!

Every Christian has received that awesome power, the same power that raised Jesus from the dead by virtue of their baptism. I believe that the time is long overdue for every Christian to use God's power. I believe that if there is such a most urgent time for the power of God to be unleashed in this world, it is NOW!

I have received some testimonies, which I believe are in the realm of the miraculous. I give praise and glory to the Lord Jesus Christ who is the King of Kings and the Lord of Lords, and the Divine Physician.

Testimonials
About the Gift of Miracles
and Working of Miracles

Dear Lennie and Ethelyn,

I just wanted to thank you and share with you about a few miracles resulting from the Charismatic Conference this past weekend attended by over 1,200 people.

All the boys from Luke 15 Prayer Group told me they had wonderful experiences at the conference. One who is a Punjabi said he really felt peace for the first time in his life and is convinced that Jesus will save and heal him; another said he was impressed by the tremendous faith of all the people gathered, and that he also grew in his faith because of that and for the first time felt like he belonged to a family—a family of Jesus; another said he realized the terrible effects of sin, and how we can simply turn to Jesus who loves us so much!

But one in particular was a more dramatic miracle: his name is Brandon. I was laying hands on him when Bob Canton came to pray over him so I witnessed it firsthand. As soon as Bob saw him, he said to him, "today you are healed from your addiction," without knowing anything about him. And immediately Brandon went down to the floor. When he woke up, he said he saw Jesus bathed in bright light, and He told him that He had been waiting for him for a very long time, and that he was so happy to have him back! He said that everyone standing in line to be blessed and prayed over by Bob and Mary Healy were actually in line on the way to Heaven!

I met Brandon today, and he told me that he received so much love from Jesus and so much understanding (in those few seconds—but it seemed like eternity to him). He is seeing everything in the world differently ever since. He has so much love in him he wants to just love and hug everybody. He also said he had a vision last night. Jesus brought to him a seventeen-year-old young boy named Ed, who attends Broadway church and is struggling with addiction, and Jesus asked him to pray for him.

One more thing—another boy, Luke, from the house who got baptized at Easter and was very close to me but then relapsed and has been on the streets, came back to the house today. For me this is a huge miracle because it's been more than four months since we saw him last and I prayed especially for him at the conference. I made a special petition in the box for him, and this is how Jesus showed me that He answered my prayer: I was driving to Luke 15 House to pray the Rosary (I do this every Monday), and I saw Luke walking towards the house. I picked him up and drove him the rest of the way. Jesus wanted me to be a part of his return and put me on the same road at that moment! Praise and glory to God!

There is no question that all nine boys who came received great healing and blessings because today when we prayed the Rosary, they prayed with so much conviction, that it almost felt as if the walls were shaking! I got the feeling that it was exactly the same way that the apostles prayed in the upper room after the Holy Spirit descended on them!

God is awesome! The conference was awesome! Dr Healy—wow! And Bob—also wow!

Glory and praise to Him forever!

Love and blessings,

Inez Vincent

Vancouver, BC, Canada

Dear Brother Bob,

It has taken me quite a long time to give you a written testimony of the miracle that I had received on March 25, 2005, at Santa Lucia Church in El Paso, Texas. I did tell you in person when you visited Las Alas in El Paso for the second time. So here's my written testimony:

I was diagnosed as having Multiple Sclerosis (MS) in April 2002. On March 25, 2005, you came to conduct a workshop and Healing Services in Santa Lucia Church. You called for people who had illnesses, and I was among those who came up for prayers. My body had always been sore and stiff.

You laid hands on me, and I rested in the Spirit. I was able to get up on my own minutes later without any assistance. This was amazing considering that my daughters would pull me up every time I would get up from the couch, and my husband would usually roll me out of bed. But this was not all. The following day, when I attended your workshop, I was able to follow your teachings and also I was able to take notes. This was really amazing because before you prayed and laid hands on me in Jesus' Name, because of MS, I could not think straight, I could not spell even simple words like what, that, and, were, and other "first-grader words." Also, I could not retain nor comprehend what I had just read a few minutes before. I would often have to ask my family to spell something out for me or to read instructions for me. On the second day of the workshop, the Lord started to heal me, but I didn't realize it right away. Before the Healing Service that evening, I was washing my hands. I looked at my face in the mirror and I had discovered a change in my face! There was a glow in my eyes that had not been there for a long time. After you prayed over me that evening and you rebuked the spirit of MS in the Name of Jesus, I again went down backward to the floor. I had nothing but peace in my heart while I was lying on the floor. Before I left for home that night after the Healing Service, I went inside the restroom again. When I checked my face in the mirror for the second time, I had noticed that even my complexion was no longer pale and haggard looking but youthful and vibrant in appearance. My cheeks had a rosy color, and my lips were no longer blue but they appeared pinkish in color. When I got home that evening, my husband did notice something in me, which he speculated as *something that resulted after a feeling of exuberance* from the seminar and Healing Service. However, when my husband had looked at my feet, which were usually blue but had now become a beautiful pink color, and my purple-looking hands that had turned reddish, youthful, soft, supple, and full of life, my husband was astonished! He says, he gets that uplifting feeling, and he became a believer in God's healing power almost overnight! I was totally healed of MS. Praise the Lord!

Thank you, Bob, for accepting God's call in leading people to their salvation in Christ Jesus. It is not only your God-given gift of healing and miracles from the Lord, but also the teachings that you imparted upon us that we should trust and rely on Jesus' loving, saving, and healing touch. Jesus is Lord!

God bless you and your family and your powerful ministry!
Sincerely,
Aileen G. Posadas
El Paso, Texas

In the early part of 2017, during my regular physical checkup, my doctor told me that he detected a heart murmur in my heart. He told me that since I was getting older, it was just a natural part of the aging process. He asked me to make sure to mention this heart murmur to my cardiologist.

When I did see the cardiologist a few months later, he confirmed that he also detected a heart murmur and he scheduled me for a sonogram of my heart. Meanwhile, I read a booklet titled, *God's Healing Light*. I read in this booklet that God loves us so much that He created us in His likeness and in His perfect image. I also got ahold of Bob Canton's book, *Miracles Never Ending*. I would pray the prayers for healing of heart problems and the "Healing and Keeping Prayer" contained in this book every morning and night, and sometimes three times a day.

While I was undergoing a sonogram in my cardiologist's office, I kept repeating and proclaiming in my mind that I was created in His perfect image and that Jesus has a perfect heart and I have a perfect heart in Jesus. I also prayed the "Healing and Keeping Prayer" in my mind since I have already memorized it.

When I went to see the cardiologist a week later for him to discuss the results of the sonogram with me, the doctor first asked me what I have been doing. I replied to him, "I have been praying a lot." My cardiologist told me that the results of the test showed that my heart is perfectly normal and that he could not find a trace of any heart problem. "As a matter of fact," my cardiologist told me, "the pictures and all the functions of your heart are better than those we took eleven years ago and are functioning much, much better now than before." Then, the cardiologist handed me the report, saying, "This is a report about your perfect heart."

I submit this testimony to affirm the tremendous power of prayer and to praise and thank God for answering my prayers. I also would like to thank Bob Canton for including those powerful prayers in his book, *Miracles Never Ending*.

Alice Orozco
Stockton, California

To Brother Bob Canton:
Last September 2018, my sister Salome Nanca Libed was diagnosed with lung cancer, stage 4. Her oncologist doctor told us that

her right lung, in between the lining, was full of small nodules or tumors, and he told us that it was too late to operate on her because the cancer had already spread to the right of her back ribs. The cancer had also spread to her liver. The oncologist suggested chemotherapy as a palliative or a last-ditch effort, but he also doubted if it could even help my sister. My sister was shocked by this bad news from the oncologist.

In the meantime, I didn't lose hope, being a member of The Children of God Prayer Community here at St. Luke's Parish in Stockton, California. I believe and trust in the power of the Lord to heal. As a member of this prayer group, I have personally witnessed so many healings over and over again during prayer meetings and Healing Services. Nothing at all is impossible for God.

Sometime in mid October 2018, I called Bob Canton to pray with my sister over the phone because she was about to see her oncologist at that time to plan for her treatment. Bob told her "not to be afraid because the Lord is healing her of her cancer." He said he had a vision of the Lord Jesus telling my sister to "trust in Him fully."

I asked my sister to attend the Mass and Healing Service in Stockton together with her prayer group members from Sacramento. My sister and her prayer group came and attended the October as well as November 2018, Mass and Healing Services. Both times, Brother Bob prayed over my sister and both times, Bob told my sister the same messages that he gave her previously: "not to be afraid and to trust in the Lord Jesus fully because He was healing her." The oncologist told my sister to get a PET scan, CT scan, and X-ray again and also to have another biopsy in early November 2018.

At the same time, the chemotherapy for my sister was scheduled to start on December 13, 2018. My sister was really perturbed and visibly depressed. She said that what the doctor told her was tantamount to a *death sentence*.

My sister and my niece and I had a meeting with the oncologist to discuss the results of all her tests on December 5, 2018. He told us that the tumors and all the cancerous cells had completely disappeared without a trace. He had no explanations as to what happened and he told my sister that "she was very lucky." He only prescribed a vitamin for her to take daily.

We told the doctor that God healed my sister as a result of prayer. He told us to "keep praying," because he said "obviously it works." My sister and my niece and I were so happy to hear the good news, and we were jumping up and down. It was a miracle! We could not stop thanking Jesus for healing my sister! It was *doom and gloom* that seemed to surround us but suddenly there was *a great light* and *great rejoicing* that followed. Jesus is alive indeed, and He gives us life! Praise God. Amen, amen!

Thank you Brother Bob and the Children of God Prayer Community for the best Christmas that we received from the Lord so far because of all your prayers and support for us. Thank you all and God bless!

Iner Nanca Pugat
Sacramento, California

Dear Bob,

I want to share with our brothers and sisters what happened to me a little over a month ago.

On August 30, 2018, during my office visit with my doctor, Dr. Li, he told me to lie down on the clinic bed. Then she did a procedure and took pictures of my throat. She showed me the pictures she took during the procedure, and I saw three tumors on the right of my throat, one big one and two small ones. On the left side of my throat, there were two tumors, one big one and one small one. Dr. Li told me she was very concerned with the two big tumors.

When I was in the car on my way home, I was extremely worried and very sad. I immediately thought of you. I reached out to you for help me with my health problem. I told you what happened. I asked you to pray with me over the tumors in my throat.

On September 6, was my next office visit. I was caught in a big surprise. The doctor asked me to sign a paper authorizing her to perform a biopsy. For the biopsy, my husband was in the room with us. He was in tears when he saw on the screen the tumors and saw the doctor performing the biopsy. After the biopsy procedure, the doctor told me to make an appointment in two weeks to discuss the result of the biopsy.

I was extremely scared of what the result might be. I called you and asked if we could pray again. I felt better after we prayed.

One day before September 20, I tried reaching out to you. You called me but, unfortunately, your cell phone was out of juice, so you had to recharge it. I waited for your call, and finally you called at 11:30 P.M. I was a bit embarrassed because it was almost midnight.

I was so happy we were able to pray again, and I want to thank you for praying with me and for me.

While waiting for the result of the biopsy, I had no appetite to eat nor a desire to do anything. My husband was so worried about me. On September 20, while my husband was driving me to the doctor's office, I told myself, submit yourself to the Lord. When we arrived at the doctor's office, the doctor met me with a big smile and said, "Maria, I have very good news for you. The tumors were all BENIGN."

I was so happy when I found out that the five tumors were all BENIGN. I gave the doctor a big hug. All of this I owe to our Lord and Savior Jesus Christ and to your Healing Ministry, Bob. Thank you so much, Bob. This is a MIRACLE. The Holy Spirit touched me with His healing power in Jesus' Name, our Lord. AMEN.

Sincerely yours,
Sally Pratt
San Jose, California

Hi Brother Bob,

I met you in New Brunswick, Canada, at the annual summer conference at Mount Allison University. I am from Prince Edward Island, and we know Gérard from our church, and he helped us make arrangements to meet with you in private. I am the lady who had cancer treatment. Last February, I had a tumor removed from my brain. Doctors got it all but it was cancerous. You prayed for me as I was still so scared, and you commanded all cancerous cells to disappear in Jesus' Name. You also commanded the anxiety and fear to leave me by imploring the Precious Blood of Jesus. You told me that you had a vision of Jesus touching my head, saying to me, "Trust in my love for you, my daughter, and do not be afraid because I am with you."

I had two scans done just three weeks ago; an MRI and a CT scan. The results came back and show no more trace of cancer. I am overjoyed and I feel blessed that they came back great, and my heart is dancing again. I keep on thanking the Lord Jesus every day.

Bob, please continue to pray for me and for my family. I claim that I'm cancer-free in Jesus' Name.

I continue to pray your "Healing and Keeping Prayer, " and my husband and son also do the same daily. We are really blessed to have met you because you are so humble yet the Lord is using you powerfully. We look forward to seeing you again. I wouldn't miss it.

You also prayed for my daughter and her husband who had been trying to conceive for a long time. I'm happy to tell you that my daughter is now in the family way. So, I wanted to tell you all the great things that the Lord has done for us. I so enjoyed that weekend of the Conference and I felt sad that it ended.

Thank you for everything you did for us. You are always in our prayers and in our hearts.

God bless you!

Cheryl Doherty

Sackville, New Brunswick, Canada

Dear Robert Canton;

I am a retired U.S. Navy Chief Petty Officer. I used to abuse my body by drinking too much alcohol and smoking three and one-half packs of cigarettes a day.

For many years, I was what they call *a lost sheep*. To make a long story short, the Lord found me and called me to work for His glory. With the Lord's help, I was able to quit smoking and drinking. However, I found out a few months after retirement that my stomach had been damaged permanently. All my smoking and drinking had worn a hole between my stomach and esophagus resulting in a hiatal hernia.

There is no cure for this ailment except maybe surgery, in which a surgeon will open a person's chest (as much as in open heart surgery). As an alternative, doctors might only provide medication to neutralize the acid in the person's stomach and into their chest cavity. This can create pain similar to a heart attack. I had this condition for three years until I attended the National Catholic Charismatic Conference in Ft. Lauderdale, Florida, sponsored by the National Service Committee of the Catholic Charismatic Renewal.

When I arrived in Ft. Lauderdale, I didn't unpack my baggage until late Friday night. It was then that I discovered that I had forgotten my medications. That night, I really suffered. I found some Rolaids and that allowed me to feel well enough to eat. Jacob, my friend and prayer partner, told me that he had sensed that I would receive a healing during this conference. On Saturday afternoon, I decided to attend the Filipino Mini Conference instead of going to my designated workshop. I needed to go to the Filipino Mini Conference so that I could report back to all the Filipino members of our prayer group in Jacksonville, Florida.

In that conference, I felt such a great outpouring of God's love. I had tears in my eyes. After the group sang a few praise and worship songs to the Lord, Robert Canton from Stockton, California, came forward to give a prophecy or a message from the Lord. Using the Holy Spirit gift of the Word of Knowledge, Bob began calling out the healings that the Lord was doing. After calling out at least five healings, Bob said that the Lord Jesus was healing a person with hiatal hernia. I raised my hand, and Bob then asked me to step into the aisle. Robert raised his right hand and pointed at me, saying, "In Jesus Name, receive your healing right now!" I fell down and I experienced what they call 'resting in the Spirit' or 'dormition.' I felt an overwhelming peace in my heart while I was lying down on the floor. That Saturday night, I slept like a baby and woke up fully refreshed. I have not needed even one Rolaid since that time, and I'm free of my medication! I'm fully healed, praise be to God! It was one miracle I will never ever forget. The Lord is wonderful and great, and I praise Him for His healing and miraculous touch. It's true! Jesus is alive forever and ever!

Terry Collins
Atlantic Beach, Florida

Hello,

My name is Rubi Nava from McMinnville, Oregon. I have five children. My oldest one just recently experienced healing when Brother Bob Canton prayed over her at Mt. Angel Community Festhalle. Guadalupe, known as Lupita, was deaf mute and was also blind in her right eye. She was able to see instantly and started hearing and sounding out words after Bob was done praying for her. In addition, four years ago to be exact, in September 2014, my husband and my family attended a retreat at Anaheim Convention Center, where Bob also prayed over our two-year-old daughter, Cindy Vargas Nava. She was diagnosed with spina bifida and her spinal column was not straight, but after the retreat we took her for her follow-up appointment, and the doctor said her spinal column was straight and could not explain what had happened. My daughter was born fine, but at the age of one month, she was diagnosed with spina bifida. I am very thankful to our Lord for all of the wonderful healings He has performed with my two daughters through the prayers of Bob Canton. We will glorify the name of Jesus forever and ever, as He continues to do miracles just like He did over 2,000 years ago.

Thanks be to God the almighty!

Rubi Nava

McMinville, Oregon

KUCHING–From 6-9 May, there was a Healing Crusade at Blessed Sacrament Church (Stampin) with Bob Canton from California (the United States of America), a lay person with a very anointed Healing Ministry.

Amongst his various ministries, Bob is a Council Member of the International Catholic Charismatic Renewal Services (ICCRS) based in the Vatican. As Divine Providence would have it, Bob had just attended a Colloquium in Rome in early April (organised by the ICCRS) on the Ministry of Deliverance and Exorcism. Fresh from this meeting in Rome, Bob came to Kuching, and the Lord demonstrated also the powerful use of the charisms of the Holy Spirit.

The crusade began with a retreat for the Emmaus Community on 6 May. The next day, there was a workshop on Effective Prayer for Deliverance, which was attended by over 700 participants, including Bishop Dominic Su from Sibu. This session was only open to selected participants.

On 8 and 9 May, Bob continued with a workshop on Effective Prayer, Charism and Evangelisation, which was attended by about 850 participants from all over Sarawak, including Bau, Serian, Bunan Gega, Sarikei, Sibu, and Miri.

Running simultaneously was the Healing Rally on the three nights of 7-9 May, starting with Mass. People attended each night for three nights, including those who are outside of the church public address system. Bob was assisted by Bishop Dominic Su (the first two nights) and Fr Lawrence Chua, Rector of Blessed Sacrament Parish, and the healing team from the Emmaus Community. On the last night, Bob specially called the youths to give their hearts and lives to Jesus, and many came forward for prayer. Looking at the sheer number of people who needed prayer for healing and deliverance it cannot be denied that the people of God are a wounded people, desperately needing the healing touch of their Shepherd. They came in spite of the rain, the crowds, the parking problems, and many other inconveniences because, evidently, they saw a chance to be touched by Jesus Christ through the ministry of Bob.

One of the healing testimonies came from eight-year-old Rosalynn Mutheardy of Kuching. Having had a lump in her left rib area since she was six months old, she attested to being healed: "Br Bob told us that Jesus is healing all the lumps. Then, Br Bob asked us to touch the lump. Mine was gone! There is no more lump and no more pain!"

There were various other healings too numerous to mention such as the blind able to see, the deaf able to hear, the paralyzed walking again, and people who were attacked by evil spirits received deliverance in the Name of Jesus, through His precious Blood. Jesus is truly the Healer of mind, body, soul, and spirit.

Christina Eng
Emmaus Community
Sarawak, Kuching Malaysia

I had near-sightedness developed a few years ago. I usually need eyeglasses to see far objects, especially at night because I am near-sighted. I attended the SCRC Convention in the Anaheim Convention Center on August 31–Sept. 2, 2018. On

Sunday, September 2, I attended the workshop conducted by Bob Canton on "Jesus, I Need Your Healing Touch." There were approximately over 1,500 people who attended the workshop. After giving his talk, Bob announced that the Lord Jesus wanted him to pray for the healing of eyes. He then asked those who had problems with their eyes or eyesight to take out their eyeglasses and place their hands on their eyes. Bob then prayed the healing prayer for the eyes. After this, he asked those who had eye problems to look around to check on their vision. When he asked how many people noticed the improvements of their eyesight, there were more than seventy people who raised their hands, including me. I noticed right away the vast improvements of my vision. My vision was very much sharper than before, and I could see clearly from far away after Bob had prayed with the congregation, praise the Lord!

As I was driving back home from Anaheim, California, after the conference, I noticed that I was able to see road signs without any problem, even from far away without glasses.

I do feel that I have brand new eyes given by the Lord! I keep thanking the Lord for this healing. Now I don't have any need to wear my eyeglasses again.

I thank you also Bob Canton for your healing prayers! God bless you and your ministry!

I am in the Modesto area and I would like to attend your prayer services in the Stockton area. Please let me know the time and venue. I would like to see you again, and perhaps I could give the testimony of my healing personally."

Blessings in Christ!
Ofelia Gallegos
Modesto, California

Bob,

Words can't express what a privilege it was to meet you. I thank you for being such a humble servant of God. When I attended the Charismatic Conference in Charleston, WV, I really had no idea what to expect. I witnessed numerous physical and spiritual healings in the name of Jesus. I was able to experience God working through you.

My mother asked you to pray for my son, Aiden who was legally blind in his left eye. About a year ago, Aiden started suddenly complaining of dizziness. He would cry every day and beg me to take him to the doctor or emergency room so someone could tell him what was wrong with him. I made him an eye appointment because I was sure that any physician would want to rule out vision problems first. The eye doctor told me that Aiden had almost no vision in his left eye. It was 20/300. He was shocked that Aiden could even play on his basketball league because he said he had no depth perception. We asked Aiden if he had ever noticed that he couldn't see out of his left eye and he told us that he didn't think he was supposed to see out of his left eye because he wasn't left-handed! Oh how children's minds work! We traveled to Johns Hopkins for two visits, and the doctors told us that we only had a narrow window of time to try and improve Aiden's vision, but that he would always need glasses or one contact for the bad left eye. Aiden has been patching his good eye to try and get his brain to better use the left eye for several months and wearing glasses. His vision with glasses has gradually improved.

Two weeks ago, Aiden saw his eye doctor at West Virginia University, and we were told that his vision with his glasses had improved to 20/25 but he was to continue to patch, and we were again told that he would need glasses for the rest of his life.

You and those in attendance at the conference prayed over Aiden for healing of his left eye on Saturday. I and many others felt strongly that a healing took place. On Monday following the conference, I called to make him an eye appointment to have his vision checked and confirm the healing. My mom had to take him for the visit, because I was working. She was a little hesitant when I told her to make sure and tell the doctor about the conference and the healing. She thought the doctor would think we were crazy.

I am so very thankful to report that the doctor checked his vision and WITH GLASSES his vision had improved to 20/20, and WITHOUT GLASSES, it was 20/25! The most amazing part was that the doctor told us in three months he feels Aiden may not need to wear glasses ever again! The doctor explained to Aiden that he believes that God heals and that He uses people in healing ministry and doctors to assist Him. What a blessing that the doctor was a believer as well!

I am so grateful that our paths crossed, Bob. You will forever be in our hearts and prayers. We will continue to praise God for his miracles!

Love and blessings to you,
Lindsay Jenkins, DDS.
Charleston, West Virginia

Robert with Aiden, a six-year- old boy who was legally blind in the left eye since birth. Aiden received a healing in his left eye during the West Virginia Catholic Charismatic Convention in Charleston, West Virginia in August 2018.

Hi Bob Canton,

First of all, I would like to thank you for your friendship. God has blessed you with many gifts. A very special gift is the gift of humility. You remain simple and very down to earth. I really enjoy going to your healing services in Stockton. Sometimes I ask myself, if God is everywhere, why I feel the need to drive to Stockton to your healing service in St. Luke's Parish every month, which is two hours away from Gridley. I feel the presence of God in your group in a very powerful way, and I feel very much welcomed.

I also learned through your teachings the importance of forgiving and loving others, even our worst enemies, as an ingredient to healing. Please continue to give teachings during the healing services. I really learned a lot by listening to you. People do need to hear anointed teachings. Your music ministry is also very anointed. How I wish we had a music ministry like yours.

My sister, Connie Ramos, received a very special healing, thanks to your prayers. A few days before the healing service in Stockton last month, Connie had chest pains. The doctors said she had some blocked arteries. She was scheduled for more tests on February 18, two days after the Healing Service of February 16.

During the healing service in Stockton on February 16, you called out a healing of hearts. You said that the Lord was healing people with heart problems. My sister came forward for prayers. You commanded the blockages in my sister's heart to be dissolved in Jesus' Name. You also told my sister to trust fully in the Lord and not to worry because He is taking care of her. Two days later, the doctor went in to see the blocked arteries. He was surprised to see that none of her artieries had any blockages, and everything appeared very normal and healthy. That was not what the doctor had seen a few days before. He said he could not explain to us what happened. He was at a loss for words. It was truly a miracle!

A lady named Ana Lucia Chavoya, whom I met in a prayer group in Gridley, was also healed. When she gave her testinony during our prayer meeting, she said that her illness was affecting her family members. Our prayer group member told me a couple of weeks ago the lady gave her testimony and was very thankful to God because she was told by the doctor that she was cancer-free, and it was also something the doctor could not explain. Late last year, she came with me to Stockton, and you and some members of your prayer group prayed over her. Thank you so much for teaching people to believe and to trust in God in all circumstances, even the seemingly hopless ones, for with God nothing is impossible at all.

Your friend,
Alma Ramos
Gridley, California

Prayer to Receive the Gift of Miracles

Father in Heaven, I give you glory
and praise and honor and worship!
Thank you for sending your Holy
Spirit in the mighty Name
of your son,
our Lord Jesus Christ.
I ask you, Father in Heaven,
to grant me the charism
of miracles for the greater glory of
the Holy Trinity.
Use me wherever I may be to draw
people unto yourself and to your
Kingdom. I want to serve you in
the realm of the miraculous for the
building up of your people and for
your greater glory and honor.
I ask this in the Mighty Name
of your Son,
our Lord Jesus Christ, Amen.

WORD GIFTS
CHAPTER 10
The Gift of Prophecy

*To one is given
through the Spirit...;
to another prophecy;...
—1 Corinthians 12:8–10—*

The Gift of Prophecy—A gift by which the Lord, using a person, speaks a message to an individual or to groups of believers gathered in a certain place. It is the Holy Spirit making use of someone to state what He thinks about the present situation, what His intention is for the future, or what He thinks they should know or be mindful of now. Prophecy may foretell the truths of God.

A prophecy that foretells relates a message that does not necessarily pertain to the things in the future.

An example of this kind of prophecy is found in 1 Corinthians 14:1, where St. Paul says:

Pursue love, but strive eagerly for the spiritual gifts, above all that you may prophesy.

In Acts 2:17–18, we read about Peter standing up with the Eleven and reiterating what the prophet Joel had prophesied:

> It will come to pass in the last days, God says,
>   that I will pour out a portion of my spirit upon all flesh.
> Your sons and your daughters shall prophesy,
>   your young men shall see visions,
>   your old men shall dream dreams.
> Indeed, upon my servants and my handmaids
>   I will pour out a portion of my spirit in those days,
>   and they shall prophesy.

To prophesy means to speak or sing a message from God under the unction or direction of the Holy Spirit. Simply put, to prophesy is to be a spokesperson for God. However, not all who prophesy are prophets, but all prophets must prophesy. Some who are called into the prophetic office by the Lord are continually using the gift of prophecy and other gifts of revelation such as the word of wisdom, word of knowledge, and discernment of spirits, in their lives and ministries.

Another example of a prophecy that foretells is when Jesus, from the Cross, told the good thief: "Amen, I say to you, today you will be with me in Paradise" (Luke 23:43).

On the other hand, foretelling relates to the things or circumstances that will come to pass in the future. An illustration of this is found in Acts 11:28:

> ...and one of them named Agabus stood up and predicted by the Spirit that there would be a severe famine all over the world, and it happened under Claudius.

By the grace of God, I have been a recipient of this type of prophecy that foretells about the future.

After my wife Chita and I experienced the baptism in the Holy Spirit back on November 11, 1984, we started to pray together. On December 8, 1984, while we were praying, my wife started prophesying:

> My son, do not be afraid. My name is Jesus and I'm talking to you through your wife. I'm going to use you to heal millions in my Name. Believe, my son, that this will happen and be humble always. You will preach the gospel in my Name. Many will come to ask for healing. Heal them in my Name because healing is good news. You will travel far and wide. You set the limits as to how far you want to go and where you want to go. You may find this hard to believe but remember, for me, nothing is impossible at all.

Soon after, I asked Chita what had prompted her to say those words to me. She said, "I only repeated what I heard the Lord was saying in my 'inner being.'" To date, I have been to fifty-one countries all over the world, preaching and proclaiming the Gospel and healing the sick in the Name of Jesus, in spite of my many limitations.

The Lord had opened the doors for me to start traveling and ministering internationally in the year 1991, exactly seven years after I received the prophecy about the works that the Lord wanted me to do for Him and for His Kingdom in His Name.

In early July 2012, my wife and I went to visit our relatives in the Philippines. When we were in Manila, I went to see then Archbishop Jose Antonio "Chito" Tagle to pay a courtesy call to him in his office. I was accompanied by my brother-in-law, Attorney Abelardo Luzano from Quezon City. The Alliance of Filipino Catholic Charismatic Prayer Communities in North America, in which I serve as the Overall National Coordinator, had Archbishop Tagle as a guest speaker during many of our national and regional conferences and conventions.

While talking with Archbishop Tagle, the Lord gave me a sense that he would be named as a Cardinal late that year. The Lord also nudged me to give this prophecy to him in the presence of my brother-in-law. Archbishop Tagle told me:

> Bob, that's almost impossible because the Pope usually announces the appointment of new Cardinals in the early part of the year. The Holy Father has just named new Cardinals this last February. Besides, I am not worthy to be named a Cardinal.

I replied, "the words I received from the Holy Spirit are for this year, 2012." I further told him to, "put it on the shelf," so to speak, and "if this is not from the Holy Spirit, then so be it."

Also, I said, "if this prophecy is from the Lord, this will certainly happen. And, if I were you, you should prepare and be ready." He just smiled at me and tapped my shoulder. On October 12, 2012, more than four months later, Pope Benedict XVI made an announcement naming Archbishop Tagle as one of the six Cardinals to be installed in the consistory in the Vatican on November 24, 2012.

Back in June 1985, when the Children of God Prayer Community of St. Luke's was only four months old, a very significant prophecy was delivered during the prayer meeting on a Saturday afternoon.

> My children, my name is Jesus. I love you all. I have great plans for this prayer group. Many will come; they will seek healing and restoration, and love and compassion. Heal them in my Name, tell them how much I love them, how much I long for them to come to me. My children, you will see great and mighty things in your prayer group. I want you to serve one another with love in my name. Remember, I will never leave you nor forsake you. Rely on me always.

In the early days of our prayer group, a person was in charge of writing down the prophecies spoken during the prayer meeting.

With great humility and with utmost thanksgiving in my heart to the Lord, I will venture to say that this prophecy has been fulfilled and is still being fulfilled to this day.

On November 14–18, 2013, the Vatican-based International Catholic Charismatic Renewal Services (ICCRS) held in Bethlehem, the Holy Land, an international meeting of two hundred ten key leaders of the Catholic Charismatic Renewal around the world. It was called the International Prophetic Consultation, and attendance was by invitation only. The meeting was not a conference rather a *prophetic consultation* to pray together and seek the Lord's will for the Renewal, especially as we were approaching our fiftieth anniversary in 2017. It was a very powerful meeting.

One evening after the meeting, we had Mass and adoration of the Blessed Sacrament followed by a praise and worship session. Then, I received words of prophecy or a message from the Lord in my heart, which I spoke out to the people gathered.

> I want you, my people, to empower the faint hearted, the weak, the discouraged. Empower them with my love, with my wisdom, and with my power, the power of my Spirit. Do it with boldness; do it with my words; do it with my vision; not with your own myopic vision, but with my vision, which can see far beyond any natural human eye can see. Do it with the vision of my Spirit. Rely on my Spirit and obey Him. I say again, rely solely on my Spirit and not with only your human power and knowledge and strength. Expand your horizons, expand your territories. Do not limit as to what I can or will do because I have no limits. There is no more time to waste. Many have fallen on the wayside because no one had cared for them or had looked after them or had shepherded them. The times are urgent. Would you heed my voice? Would you heed my call?

Thank God that someone had tape-recorded the session, and he passed the recorded message on to me.

A prophecy may also come forth through someone who speaks in "tongues." In 1 Corinthians 14:5, St. Paul says:

Now I should like all of you to speak in
tongues, but even more to prophesy. One who
prophesies is greater than one who speaks
in tongues, unless he interprets, so that the
church may be built up.

When someone speaks in tongues in a prayer meeting,
for instance, the gift of interpretation of tongues should
also be operative to make the message in tongues un-
derstandable to the hearers. The person who is speaking
in tongues may give the interpretation under the inspiration of the Holy Spirit, or somebody else in the congregation may be prompted to do it. It should be noted
that interpretation is not necessarily a translation of the
message delivered through speaking in tongues. (Please
see the Chapter on the Gift of Interpretation of Tongues
for more information.)

How to Hear the Voice of God
The Lord wants to talk to us and He is always speaking
to us. In the book of Genesis, we read these words many
times: "Then God said,". In John 10:27, Jesus says: "My
sheep hear my voice; I know them, and they follow me."
Jesus also says:

Amen, I say to you, many prophets and righ-
teous people longed to see what you see but
did not see it, and to hear what you hear but
did not hear it (Matthew 13:17).

Our God wants to have fellowship with us. Jesus died
on the Cross for us not only to set us free from the bondage of sin and death, but also to bring us to a person-

al relationship and fellowship with Him. The Lord is more delighted to speak to us than we are to hear from Him. Most of the time, the Lord communicates with us through a still small voice from within our spirit. A person may perceive it as a sudden impression, or *a sense* of something that God is saying, or *a passing thought*. If we open ourselves, our hearts, our senses, and our minds to God, and are obedient to Him, we will surely hear His voice. The Lord can give us an impression, or a vision, or a thought. He can also communicate with us through dreams, through scriptures, through our circumstances, through other people, and even through His audible voice, which is very rare indeed. He is sovereign and He has no limitations.

Sometime in the fall of 2009, the members of the Executive Board of the Empowered 21 held a meeting in Los Angeles, California. Empowered 21 is an organization that focuses on shaping the future of the Global Spirit-empowered movement by focusing on crucial issues facing the movement and connecting generations for intergenerational blessing and impartation.

Among those present in the meeting were Bill Wilson, currently the president of Oral Roberts University in Tulsa, Oklahoma; Vinson Synan, former Director of the Holy Spirit Resource Center of Oral Roberts University; Cindy Jacobs, author, speaker, teacher, and evangelist and who is listed in *Who's Who Among American Women;* Samuel Rodriguez, Director of the National Hispanic Christian Leadership Conference; Jack Hayford, Pentecostal minister and author; and Oreste Pesare, Director of the Vatican-based International Catholic Charismatic Renewal Services (ICCRS); and yours truly as Council member of ICCRS representing North America, Central America, and Caribbean countries; and others with different ministries in their own rights.

As we opened the meeting with prayers, then followed with praise and worship, I received a mental picture or vision of throngs of angry people up in arms, shouting at the top of their voices. Then, there were bombs exploding, armies firing guns, and tanks, heavy artilleries, and thousands of people dead on the streets. Then the Lord spoke into my heart. He said:

> My son, troubles will come in the Middle East. Many governments will be toppled down, violence will be pervasive, and many will lose their lives. Tell your brothers and sisters to pray, to fast, and to intercede for the people in the Middle East so that peace will reign.

I shared this vision and the prophecy with those who were attending this meeting.

In December 2010, the Arab spring started in the Middle East, about one and one-half years after I received the prophecy from the Lord. By the end of February 2012, rulers had been forced from power in Tunisia, Egypt, Libya, and Yemen; civil uprisings had erupted in Bahrain and Syria; major protests had broken out in Algeria, Iraq, Jordan, Kuwait, Morocco, Oman, and Sudan; and minor protests had occurred in Mauritania, Saudi Arabia, and other countries in the Middle East.

I remember one time when I had a very difficult problem to solve. I really agonized to find the solution or solutions to this particular problem. I really needed the Lord's wisdom and guidance more than anything else.

At that time, I was still working as a senior auditor-appraiser for the San Joaquin County Assessor's office in Stockton, California. During my morning break, I immediately ran to St. Mary's Church, which was one block away from my office, to pray before the Blessed Sacrament in the church. I did the same thing during my afternoon break. I was just by myself inside the church. My prayer of desperation sounded like this:

> Lord Jesus, I praise your Name! Lord please do this, and please do that, because if you don't do this or if you don't do that, this will be like this and that would be like that.

I said the same prayer and exactly the same words morning and afternoon for three days. On Thursday morning, as I just knelt down to start my prayer, after I made the sign of the Cross, I heard a voice—an audible voice that was loud enough for me to hear yet very "gentle" and "peaceful." It had a very calming effect. I looked around and surveyed the inside of the church, and I was the only person inside. I then perceived it to be the audible voice of the Lord.

The voice said, "my son, repeat after me. Jesus, I trust in you." I repeated it, and the voice said, "again, my son." The Lord must have said it six more times, and I repeated what He said to me.

This seemingly serious problem I had was just solved without me lifting a finger. In fact, there was nothing that I could have done whatsoever to solve the problem with my own wisdom or knowledge or know-how.

A few years ago, I had the opportunity to conduct a Parish Mission in Sarasota, Florida. While giving a talk

about "Repentance and Forgiveness," the Lord spoke
into my heart that there was a person in the congregation
who tried to commit suicide and that He was setting him
free from the feelings of guilt and self-condemnation.
When I received the words, there was a deep conviction
in my heart that they came from the Lord. I announced
what the Lord had said, and a man named John came up
to the altar, with tears in his eyes, to acknowledge everything that I said. I sensed that John tried to do it not once
but twice, and he admitted it when I asked him about it.
That day, he received an emotional and spiritual healing
and an assurance that the Lord, in His mercy and love,
had not condemned rather had forgiven him.

Recently, John told me that his life had changed rapidly
for the better because he had become closer to the Lord.

In the New Testament, we read of many great prophetic utterances. Simeon prophesied about Jesus in
Luke 2:32–35:

> …and Simeon blessed them and said to Mary
> his mother, "Behold, this child is destined for
> the fall and rise of many in Israel, and to be a
> sign that will be contradicted (and you your-
> self a sword will pierce) so that the thoughts
> of many hearts may be revealed."

In Acts 13:2–3, we read about Paul and Barnabas to
be set apart for God's work.

> While they were worshiping the Lord and
> fasting, the holy Spirit said, "Set apart for me
> Barnabas and Saul for the work to which I
> have called them." Then, completing their

fasting and prayer, they laid hands on them
and sent them off.

Discernings of Spirits

There are four sources of voices that we can hear in
the spiritual realm, namely: the Holy Spirit, the human
spirit, evil spirits, and holy angels. In 1 John 4:1, the word
of God says:

> Beloved, do not trust every spirit but test the
> spirits to see whether they belong to God, be-
> cause many false prophets have gone out into
> the world.

In 1 Thessalonians 5:19–21, St. Paul says:

> Do not quench the Spirit. Do not despise
> prophetic utterances. Test everything; retain
> what is good.

Both the *giver* of the prophecy and the *receiver*, or the
hearer, should discern the words. A very careful and thor-
ough discernment must be undertaken, especially in
cases of directive prophecies to make sure that they are
from God and not from false prophets. To discern rightly
and accurately, we need the wisdom and assistance of
the Holy Spirit who "guides us to all truth." Jesus says in
John 16:13–15:

> But when he comes, the Spirit of truth, he
> will guide you to all truth. He will not speak
> on his own, but he will speak what he hears,
> and will declare to you the things that are

coming. He will glorify me, because he will
take from what is mine and declare it to you.
Everything that the Father has is mine; for
this reason I told you that he will take from
what is mine and declare it to you.

The following are some of the practical guidelines in
judging or discerning the source(s) of a prophecy:

1. It must edify or build up and give comfort.
If a prophecy is negative and condemnatory, it
is a sure sign that it is not from God (1 Thessalonians 5:11).

2. It must bear good fruit. "Every tree that
does not bear good fruit will be cut down and
thrown into the fire. So by their fruits you will
know them" (Matthew 7:19–20).

3. It must be scriptural. Jesus says: "…The
words I have spoken to you are spirit and life"
(John 6:63).

4. It must conform to the teachings of the mag-
esterium of the Catholic Church. The mages-
terium is the teaching authority of the Church.

5. It must produce peace. St.Paul says: "…
since he is not the God of disorder but of
peace…" (1 Corinthians 14:33).

6. It must ultimately bring glory and honor to
God. St. Paul states: "So whether you eat or

drink, or whatever you do, do everything for the glory of God" (1 Corinthians 10:31).

7. It must strengthen the faith of both the giver of the prophecy and the hearer(s). "Thus faith comes from what is heard, and what is heard comes through the word of Christ." (Romans 10:17)

Testimonial
About the Gift of Prophecy

A leader of a prayer group in our area, Xochit Honorato, came to you, Bob, on October 7, 2016, for prayer. She had just lost her son earlier in the year in a tragic car accident, and she had not been the same since. She had not been able to sleep after her son was gone. She goes to work at 7:00 AM, but she said every night she would be waking up at 1:00, 3:00, and 5:00 AM with constant sleep interruptions. You prayed over her and gave her some words of prophecy that her son was telling her, "My mom, I want you to let go. Know that I am very happy where I am now because I am with the Master. Go on with life. Cry no more because I am with the Master. Do what the Master wants you to do. The Master wants you to love others as He loves you." Bob, you also told her your vision of the Lord Jesus with her son.

My dear friend, Xochit, received spiritual and emotional healing, as she is now able to sleep and has indicated she cried and cried after hearing the words her son was telling her, "Don't cry, Mother, as I am with my Master." She told me that was how her son referred to the Lord when he was still alive, as "the Master." She feels comfort and peace as she knows now that her son is in the presence of God. She is very much amazed of the prophecy that you delivered to her which was anointed by the Holy Spirit.

Now, she told me she is able to sleep all night without interruptions. She gave testimony that through brother Bob, the Lord sent her the peace she needed, and that our Lord is merciful and ever-loving.

Your words to her from the Lord have definitely soothed her aching heart. She is filled with the Lord's love now and is ready to give it to everyone around her. Thanks be to God!

Irene Flores
McMinville, Oregon

Robert praying over the attendees during the "Workshop on Spiritual Warfare and Healing" in Edmonton, Alberta, Canada, in 2013.

Prayer to Receive the Gift of Prophecy

Lord Jesus,
by the power of the Holy Spirit,
I ask you to grant me the charism
of prophecy so that I will be able
to share your message with my
brothers and sisters for their
edification and for your greater
glory and honor.
Use me, in spite of myself,
to manifest this charism
to increase my faith and that of
my fellow Christians.
I ask this in your Holy Name,
Lord Jesus, Amen.

WORD GIFTS
CHAPTER 11
The Gift of Tongues

Tongues—The ability given by the Holy Spirit to speak in a type of language not understood by the speaker. It is the Spirit of God praying within the heart of the person.

In Romans 8:26–27, St. Paul says:

> In the same way, the Spirit too comes to the aid of our weakness; for we do not know how to pray as we ought, but the Spirit itself intercedes with inexpressible groanings. And the one who searches hearts knows what is the intention of the Spirit, because it intercedes for the holy ones according to God's will.

The gift of tongues is mentioned fifty-seven times in the New Testament. Some say it is the least of the gifts, but I'm among those who believe it is a doorway to other gifts of the Holy Spirit.

I have noticed that after I was bestowed with the gift of tongues by the Holy Spirit, I also started to manifest all the other gifts such as the word of knowledge, healing, miracles, prophecy, and so forth.

In 1 Corinthians 14:2, St. Paul says:

> For one who speaks in a tongue does not speak
> to human beings but to God, for no one listens;
> he utters mysteries in spirit.

In 1 Corinthians 14:4, St. Paul says: "Whoever speaks in a tongue builds himself up,…" and in 1 Corinthians 14:18, St. Paul also says, "I give thanks to God that I speak in tongues more than any of you."

The Lord Jesus, in Mark 16:17–18, says,

> These signs will accompany those who believe:
> in my name they will drive out demons, they
> will speak new languages. They will pick up
> serpents [with their hands], and if they drink
> any deadly thing, it will not harm them. They
> will lay hands on the sick, and they will recover.

Indeed, those who believe in Jesus Christ will do the things that He did in His name.

Let us recall what took place in the Upper Room in Jerusalem on the Day of Pentecost when one hundred twenty apostles and disciples of Jesus were gathered to pray:

> When the time for Pentecost was fulfilled, they
> were all in one place together. And suddenly
> there came from the sky a noise like a strong
> driving wind, and it filled the entire house
> in which they were. Then there appeared to
> them tongues as of fire, which parted and
> came to rest on each one of them. And they

were all filled with the holy Spirit and began
to speak in different tongues, as the Spirit en-
abled them to proclaim (Acts 2:1–4).

Because of that experience with the Holy Spirit, the
lives of the apostles had been turned upside down and
inside out. They were never the same again.

I could not thank the Lord enough that, through His
Holy Spirit, He endowed me with the gift of tongues and
other gifts.

The first time I received the gift of tongues, I was attending Mass on a Sunday morning by myself because
my wife and my two children were in the San Francisco
Bay area at that time. I had been asking the Lord to grant
me this gift. When the presiding priest was praying the
"epiclesis," a prayer invoking the Holy Spirit to change
the bread and the wine into the body and blood of Jesus,
I started to babble some words. At first, it sounded like I
was saying *Abba, Alleluia*, repeated many times with a speed
faster than the speed of sound, so I thought. Then, suddenly, I felt like I was speaking in the Greek language and
tried my best to say the newly acquired gift of tongues in a
very low voice hoping that nobody could hear it. The person to my left and to my right could still hear it, however,
because they both asked me if I was okay.

I remember vividly one Saturday afternoon in the
1990s after a prayer meeting, a member of our prayer
group, Ana, from Modesto, California, a forty-minute
drive from Stockton, told us that her car's ignition would
not start. So, four of us went out to the front of the building where the prayer meeting was held to check out what
happened to Ana's car. I believe that none of us at that
time knew anything about how to fix a car, much less

how to make the ignition of a car work. We asked Ana to turn the ignition key again. She did it at least three times, but nothing worked.

I then asked everyone to join me in praying over the car and asked the Lord to empower the car to start. As we prayed, we commanded the car to start in Jesus' Name and then everybody prayed in tongues afterwards. Then, I asked Ana to turn the ignition key again. To our great exhilaration, the the engine of the car started to work. Everybody was giving thanks and praising the Lord for this miracle. Everybody was really excited, especially Ana.

We advised Ana to take her car to the repair shop to have the car checked out to make sure it was okay for her to drive to Modesto. The repair shop was about two and one-half miles away from where we were.

That evening, Ana called me to report to me that the car mechanic was really perplexed as to what happened to the car. He told Ana that the cables on the battery of the car were very, very loose, and two cables actually came off of the battery. He told her that there was "no way in the world that the car would have started."

Ana told me that she had no words to explain it to the mechanic, but that it was the work and the power of the Holy Spirit that made it happen!

This phenomenon had increased the faith of the people in our prayer group even more in the miraculous power of the Lord Jesus Christ.

In Romans 8:26–27, St. Paul says:

> In the same way, the Spirit too comes to the aid of our weakness; for we do not know how to pray as we ought, but the Spirit itself intercedes with inexpressible groanings. And the

one who searches hearts knows what is the intention of the Spirit, because it intercedes for the holy ones according to God's will.

There are three basic types of tongues, namely: tongues for prayer, tongues for speaking/interpretation, and demonic tongues.

Praying in tongues is a gift whereby the person prays to God in a language which he does not know, by simply *yielding* to the action of the Spirit. Simply put, it is offering a prayer to God or lifting up your heart and mind to God. Therefore, interpretation for this kind of tongue is not necessary.

Speaking in tongues is speaking the word of God to a congregation in the form of a prophecy, or speaking a message, from God. If one prophecies in tongues, an interpretation is, of course, needed for the congregation to understand or at least know what the message from God is all about or to understand the essence of the message from the Lord. In 1 Corinthians 14:13–14, St. Paul says:

> Therefore, one who speaks in a tongue should pray to be able to interpret. [For] if I pray in a tongue, my spirit is at prayer but my mind is unproductive.

The interpretation of tongues is not necessarily a word-for-word translation of what was spoken in tongues. However, there are some exceptions. We should never place limitations on the Holy Spirit.

One time during our prayer meeting, someone spoke in tongues. Another person, gave the interpretation of what was spoken in tongues. A third person commented

THE GIFT OF TONGUES

that the one who spoke in tongues actually spoke in the French language, and the second person interpreted what was spoken in French. These two people, the one who spoke in tongues, and the one who gave the interpretation, do not speak nor understand the French language, but the third person speaks and understands French.

This phenomenon helped boost the faith of the people in our prayer group that the Holy Spirit is indeed active among His people. (For more information regarding the Gift of Interpretation of Tongues, kindly see the next chapter about this gift.)

Demonic tongues is a language used by the evil one to mimic the Gift of Tongues from the Holy Spirit. Satan is a master counterfeiter and he counterfeits everything that is of God and from God.

At one of the Healing Crusades that I had the privilege to conduct in Las Vegas, Nevada, I prayed over a woman for healing. I usually pray in tongues while laying hands on a person. I noticed that the tone of my prayer language had turned into a *staccato* sounding kind of prayer, which is like a prayer of command adjuring the evil spirit to leave in Jesus' Name. When this happened, I knew right away that a demonic spirit was present and was oppressing the woman with whom I was praying. I likened this speech pattern as a warning signal from the Holy Spirit that an enemy was present.

The woman went down on the floor and spoke in a tongue-like sounding language while crawling like a snake. I discerned that she had a satanic or evil tongue. The words that came out of her mouth were very *harsh* and a very angry-sounding kind of language. Then she started barking like a dog. I immediately covered myself and the rest of the congregation with the Precious Blood of Jesus, through the power of the Holy Spirit, to prevent any attack and contamination on all those present. I also invoked the intercession of the Virgin Mary and St. Joseph and all the Archangels in heaven, and then prayed a deliverance prayer for the woman using the mighty Name and the Blood of Jesus.

I found out later that this woman had been heavily involved in occultism.

After she calmed down, I led her to renounce the evil one and to invite Jesus into her heart and into her life. She told me that she could not remember what she had said and what she had done. I told her I discerned that the spirits of divination and occultism, spirits of heaviness and bondage, *sleeping* spirits, spirits of mockery, and lying spirits were attacking her. I advised her to partake in the Sacrament of Confession as soon as possible, to go to Mass daily, and to do other spiritual exercises to cleanse and free herself completely from these oppressive spirits.

I firmly believe that the enemy cannot understand the Gift of Tongues that the Holy Spirit gives to Christian believers. It is even safe to say that the evil one is afraid of a Christian who prays and speaks in tongues.

St. Paul, in 1 Corinthians 14:2, says,

> For one who speaks in a tongue does not speak to human beings but to God, for no one listens; he utters mysteries in spirit.

Basically, there are two kinds of tongues, namely praying in tongues and speaking in tongues. Praying in tongues, of course, doesn't need an interpretation because it is a prayer language that an individual utters to

God alone. Speaking in tongues, of course, does need an interpretation, because it is given by the Holy Spirit to the congregation in a form of a prophecy or a message.

I have noticed many times that when I speak in tongues, the words that I utter are quite different than when I pray in tongues. Sometimes, the Holy Spirit will give me the interpretation of the tongues that I speak before the congregation in the English language. As a result, I also give the interpretation as well for everybody in the congregation to understand the message from the Lord. Otherwise, somebody else in the conregation will give the interpretation of tongues through the leadings and promptings of the Holy Spirit. (See the chapter on Gift of Interpretation of Tongues.)

SIDEBAR FEATURE
"How I learned to speak in tongues and how you can too"
by Jeff Mazzone
Originally written for and published by Catholic365.com on 09/07/2016.

When I was a college seminarian, I heard of people speaking in tongues, but I knew very little about it. I thought it was pretty whacky and folks who did it a little loopy. But ten years ago, my two-week application visit with the religious order I would join a few months later changed my ideas on tongues, and put me on the road to discovering and receiving the God-given gift for myself.

I came to know the Franciscan Friars of the Renewal quite well before I applied to join them. They were crazy, but I certainly did not think they were whacky or loopy. The Feast of Pentecost fell during that application visit, and the friars and sisters were holding a public festival of praise the evening before. What I experienced that night completely rocked my world.

I saw the superior general of the friars, who stood about six-foot eight, waving his hands in the air, dancing, singing, and praying…in tongues. Complete jibberish. I had never heard anything like it. Then I saw a brother and two sisters from England, who to me exemplified what I believed was the height of English propriety, doing the same. All of them were utterly free, totally abandoned, and filled with joy. This was the closest thing I had ever seen that could compare to the story of David dancing naked before the Ark of the Covenant, disregarding the shame his misunderstanding wife felt in her embarrassment over her husband exposing himself in the city streets.

And then there was me. A little freaked out and trying to balance my previous notions of whacky and loopy with the respect and admiration I held for these people.

After I joined the community, I heard a friar giving a talk on tongues. He related it to baby talk. Babies cannot communicate what they want or feel, but they make noises in an effort to do so. Those noises have no boundaries, rules, grammar, or structure. They just flow freely. Likewise, just as the sweetest sounds to a parent are the little coos his or her child makes, so are our little noises before the Father. When I come home from work, I feel pure joy when my five-month-old daughter smiles and makes her little noises upon seeing my face for the first time since the night before.

In the Gospel, we hear Jesus say "Unless you turn and become like children, you will never enter the kingdom of heaven" (Mt. 18). The greek word there is not "children" like an eight-year-old, but is actually infant. Unless you become like an infant, you cannot enter the Kingdom of Heaven. We need to be dependent on the Father like an infant depends on its parents. Likewise, we remember the psalm, "You whose glory above the heavens is chanted by the mouth of babes and infants" (Ps. 8). Perhaps praying like an infant before the Father is a type of praise we can render.

Speaking in tongues, he said, is an experience of free and boundless prayer that is unconventional, unpracticed, unsophisticated, unsystematic, and unformulated. While we rationally guide when and how we use the gift once we have discovered and received it, the gift itself is an experience of freedom from the mechanics of language that often clog our wheels; it frees us from the moments when we cannot find the right words to express what we are thinking or feeling. Furthermore, this form of prayer helps overcome the mental obstacles that often arise when trying to pray "the right way" while praying in silence, yet still leads us to the end goal of the silent contemplation we struggle to reach.

Now a little Scriptural catechesis. C'mon Catholics; dust off those Bibles–let's go.

St. Paul describes in 1 Corinthians 14 what could be seen as an ancient charismatic prayer meeting. He addresses the dynamic between the gift of tongues and the gift of prophecy. I imagine St. Paul as a New Yorker because his words sound something like "Hey–you guys speaking in tongues? Good for you, but what good is it for everyone else? We're all supposed to speak in tongues. Come find me when you learn to prophesy. Now get outta here and quit wasting my time." St. Paul is telling us that though this is a gift that only comes from God; it is also a gift that everyone should have already received and should be using regularly.

He tells us that the gift of tongues is not for speaking to men; it is for speaking to God. The gift of tongues is not for the edification, encouragement, or consolation of others; it is for the edification, encouragement, and consolation of self.

A commentary on this passage written in 1922 by the Dominican Rev. Charles J Callan, O.P. totally nailed it. He wrote:

"The gift of tongues is not for preaching or teaching, but praying to God. He edifies himself not because he knows what he is saying, but because he knows he is praising God and speaking to God in prayer, stimulating and increasing faith and love, but not helping others."

The gift of tongues stimulates and increases faith and love in the one who uses it. Turns out that those who approve of or believe in the gift of tongues are not just folks who participated in the Charismatic Renewal in the 70s and 80s, or graduates from Franciscan University of Steubenville. This priest of an order famous for its orthodoxy throughout the centuries commented positively on it forty years before Vatican II! Not exactly whacky or loopy.

By the way, did you know that the Preacher to the Papal Household–the personal preacher to Pope Francis, Pope Benedict, and Pope St. John Paul II–prays in tongues? Yup. I saw it too when I met him in New Jersey at a charismatic conference.

So back to the friars. I was in the community a year when the next class of guys joined. Two of them were visiting the friary where I was for the night, and they got into a conversation with some of the older friars about the gift of tongues. For the last few months, I had been praying for the gift to speak in tongues, but nothing was happening. I was too caught up in trying to do it right, too bound by my own fear of failure, and too worried about becoming whacky, loopy, or both.

So later that night, I sat down with those two guys and asked them, "How do you pray in tongues?"

They told me that God gives everyone the gift of tongues, but not everyone has learned to use it. They instructed me to pray against the pride, pray for openness, pray for freedom, pray like the mute man who could not speak yet managed to ask Jesus to free his tongue.

And they gave me some practical suggestions. First pray with words…then pray with syllables…and then, fasten your seatbelt.

So when I returned to my cell, I closed the door, lit a candle, knelt before my crucifix, and started praying aloud repetitively:

"Praise you, Jesus. Thank you, Jesus. Glory to you, Lord. Alleluia, alleluia, alleluia… ."

And then the monosyllabic baby talk:

"Ah…ah…ba…ah…la…ah…ba…."

And then, an explosion of sound flowed from my tightened lips like water breaking through a dam.

A wind blew through me that may not have shaken the walls of my cell, but certainly shattered the walls of my self-consciousness. I experienced what the multitude might have felt in the upper room or what happened to the mute man when Jesus freed his tongue and opened his lips.

That 1922 commentary put it lightly when it said that speaking in tongues stimulates and increases faith and love. My faith skyrocketed through the exosphere and my love burst into a conflagration that consumed my heart.

I collapsed in joy, crying and laughing.

Ten years later, I still use tongues whether in groups or in my personal prayer. I would not call myself a charismatic, but I would call myself a Catholic. One is not exclusive to the other. Don't get me wrong, nothing beats long periods of silent prayer. And not to equivocate the two, but I can pray in tongues during praise and worship with guitars just as easily as I can after receiving communion at a Mass in the extraordinary form.

Have we tapped into this gift that the Lord may have already placed in our souls? After all, gifts are meant to be used. Maybe we admire others who move in the gift but think it could never happen for us. Or perhaps we are as I was: afraid of being whacky or loopy.

For me, it is like dancing. I was terrified of dancing at weddings because I did not know how to dance. Then I married a woman from Dominican Republic. I still do not know how to dance, but now I have a ton of fun trying. I see other men watching me have fun, and I wish I could shake them from their fear…or introduce them to a nice Latina.

The Liturgy of the Hours begins with this prayer from the Psalms: "Lord, open my lips and my mouth will proclaim your praise." May the Lord open our lips that our mouths may praise Him in every way and form that He desires and not just those with which we are currently comfortable.

Bio:

Jeff Mazzone, a former diocesan seminarian and Franciscan Friar of the Renewal, received his M.A. in theology from St. Joseph's Seminary in Yonkers, NY, and is currently enrolled in an online M.A. in professional counseling through Liberty University in Lynchburg, VA. He and his wife live north of New York City with their two children. Apart from managing a charter bus company, Jeff regularly leads music at various parishes and events in the New York area.

Facebook: https://www.facebook.com/jeff.mazzone.7

SIDENOTES by Jeff Mazzone

The Pentecost account in Acts 2 tells us that "they were all filled with the Holy Spirit and began to speak in other tongues, as the Spirit gave them utterance." The Greek word for what happened at Pentecost is the same Greek word St. Paul uses when he describes in 1 Corinthians 14 what it is to speak in tongues.

Corinth was quite far from Jerusalem, and Paul writes to the Corinthians decades after the Pentecost experience in the upper room, so it is not as if the only people who received the gift of tongues were those in Jerusalem on that day. We do not know of any Pentecost-like experience in Corinth, but we do know that they were baptized and likely confirmed in an early Church form of the same sacrament we celebrate today.

The gift of tongues is one of a numberless amount of charismatic gifts, some of which are mentioned in the letters of St. Peter and St. Paul. The charismatic gifts are not like the sevenfold sanctifying gifts of the Holy Spirit that we receive fully in confirmation. The charismatic gifts do not make us holy. Instead, they help us build up the Church; they are service gifts. Nonetheless, they cannot be earned; they are instead freely given.

"I have the strength for everything through Him who empowers me."

–Philippians 4:13–

Following are a couple of testimonials regarding the Gift of Tongues.

Testimonials
About the Gift of Tongues

Dear Robert,

When I attended the Life In the Spirit seminar at Presentation Church, I was completely unaware of what to expect. I heard about the gift of tongues that weekend for the first time. And I said I didn't want it for two reasons:

1. It was fear of the unknown.

2. I believed it was a selfish gift to ask for and praising God wouldn't help other people, or so I thought.

A month later, two people within five days spoke to me about the gift of tongues. Several days after that, as I was driving home from work, I asked the Lord to grant me the gift of tongues, and I received this gift to my amazement. When I arrived home, my only thought was to praise God and thank Him for His gift. I told God I would do anything for Him. And I heard a one-word response, "Smoking." The Lord wanted me to quit smoking. How does a thirty-year veteran smoker answer? "Yes, Lord." Gift upon gift, the Lord is so generous. Quitting smoking was easy. I did not have any cravings to smoke. I did not have to go out and buy celery or gum to munch on. I could rarely smell cigarette smoke! This remains so today!

I attended the Mass and Healing Service at St. Luke's Parish. I saw how praying in tongues can be utilized to help other people. I had never been to a Mass and Healing Service before. Why didn't I realize that people would be healed during the Mass and Healing Service? Arms, legs, eyes—miracle upon miracle, blessing upon blessing.

Each and every miracle exemplified God's love and compassion for His people!
Marlene G.
Stockton, California

The weekend of the AFCCPC Baltimore Convention opened my eyes and strengthened my faith to a new level. The countless lessons learned there had the common theme of relating to that one unforgettable Bible verse. This verse, Philippians 4:13, was one direct teaching that somehow spoke to me. God called me by name to that convention for that to be imprinted in my heart, and through that one verse, all my doubts, fears, and questions were answered.

Saturday morning, BLD Washington Youth was in charge of leading morning praise. With all of the chaos and scrambling of songs, I somehow managed to listen to Father Leo Patalinghug as he reached out not only to me but also to everyone there. He mentioned the fact that not many can recognize the image of Holy. Naturally, numerous ideas of what could possibly define holiness ran through my mind. I realized that the more mysterious our God seemed to be, the more I strived to know Him. That day made me rethink my understanding of my Lord and Savior. As each lesson became instilled in us, so too was the Holy Spirit in our hearts.

After Mass, a few of the BLD Youth kids decided to stay and attend a special activity led by the Pater Noster Youth Group. Never in my wildest dreams did I expect that one night to be so overwhelming and profound. Their group did an amazing and inspiring performance that left my peers and me in awe. We saw Christ through them. We witnessed kids our age interpreting and displaying God's love to inexplicable proportions. I saw exactly what He wanted and probably needed me to see. That night was empowering, wonderful, eye-opening–baffling. That night was a glimpse of His love, and all I want is to see more of it.

After that night I felt that nothing could top such an experience; that there was probably no point in going back on Sunday because all that was left was the closing. Fortunately, BLD Youth returned that day, for I learned that there is nothing more important than closure to such an amazing experience. Brother Bob Canton, the AFCCPC Overall Coordinator led us into a healing session, having us say "Abba Alleluia." Eventually this slurred, as I slowly began to speak what he called the "language of the Holy Spirit." I cannot even begin to describe what receiving the gift of tongues feels like. Although there were others louder than I, it felt as if I were alone with God. All of my feelings that even I myself struggled to put to words were poured out that day, and for the first time, I was sure God was listening. Without this closure, I believe that all the teachings and inspiring experiences would have been left incomplete. I felt like I finally understood God; even if it was for just a brief moment.

Heavenly Father, thank you for calling me to this convention. I ask that you instill in me all the lessons that I have learned over this weekend and help me to apply them to my daily life. Continue to be my saving grace, and grant unto me the wisdom of your ways, so that I may serve you to my fullest potential. All this I pray in the name of the Father, Son, and Holy Spirit. Amen.

By making the sign of the Cross, I learned that we make ourselves targets of Christ. Yes, I realize that after this moment with God it will be hard to resist temptations. They say the closer one comes to the light, the bigger their shadow becomes. I, however, am ready to make myself an open target to God, regardless of the trials. Why? Philippians 4:13. That's why.

Anika Aquino
Washington, D.C.
BLD Chapter

Prayer to Receive
the Gift of Tongues

Father in heaven, I thank you,
I praise you, I glorify your Name.
I ask you Lord to grant me the Gift
of Tongues through the power of
your Holy Spirit in Jesus' Name.
St. James says in James 1:17,
"...all good giving and every
perfect gift is from above,
coming down from the Father
of lights, with whom there is no
alteration or shadow
caused by change."
Lord, thank you for answering my
prayer in Jesus' Name, Amen.

Robert exhorting the attendees to do the works of Jesus during the San Antonio Catholic Charismatic Conference in San Antonio, Texas, March 1-2, 2019.

Attendees of the Healing Rally in St. Isidore Catholic Church in Yuba City, California, north of Sacramento.

Robert's Healing Crusades in Malaysia attended by thousands in 2017.

Praying over the sick during the Japan Renewal Conference in Tokyo, Japan, in 2017.

WORD GIFTS
CHAPTER 12
The Gift of Interpretation of Tongues

To one is given through the Spirit...
the interpretation of tongues.
—1 Corinthians 12:8, 10—

Interpretation of Tongues—The ability given by the Holy Spirit to speak, in a language understood by the speaker and hearer(s), the meaning of words previously spoken in an unknown language.

When a person speaks in tongues during a prayer meeting or prayer assembly, this is usually a message or prophecy from God to the community. This normally takes place after the gathered assembly prays and praises God in tongues. In this setting, an interpretation of tongues is necessary for everyone in the assembly to understand the message from God.

The gift of interpretation of tongues could be described also as the ability to understand and communicate, through the power of the Holy Spirit, an incomprehensible utterance of tongues for the spiritual benefit and upbuilding of the prayer group or the gathered assembly.

In 1 Corinthians 14:6–18, St. Paul says,

> Now, brothers, if I should come to you speaking in tongues, what good will I do you if I do not speak to you by way of revelation, or knowledge, or prophecy, or instruction? Likewise, if inanimate things that produce sound, such as flute or harp, do not give out the tones distinctly, how will what is being played on flute or harp be recognized? And if the bugle gives an indistinct sound, who will get ready for battle? Similarly, if you, because of speaking in tongues, do not utter intelligible speech, how will anyone know what is being said? For you will be talking to the air. It happens that there are many different languages in the world, and none is meaningless; but if I do not know the meaning of a language, I shall be a foreigner to one who speaks it, and one who speaks it a foreigner to me. So with yourselves: since you strive eagerly for spirits, seek to have an abundance of them for building up the church.

> Therefore, one who speaks in a tongue should pray to be able to interpret. [For] if I pray in a tongue, my spirit is at prayer but my mind is unproductive. So what is to be done? I will pray with the spirit, but I will also pray with the mind. I will sing praise with the spirit, but I will also sing praise with the mind. Other-

wise, if you pronounce a blessing [with] the
spirit, how shall one who holds the place
of the uninstructed say the "Amen" to your
thanksgiving, since he does not know what
you are saying? For you may be giving thanks
very well, but the other is not built up. I give
thanks to God that I speak in tongues more
than any of you.

Various forms of interpretation of tongues can be delivered during a prayer meeting or prayer assembly:

1. It could be delivered as a word-for-word interpretation.
I, for one, have had some experiences of receiving the
interpretation of tongues. In more than one instance, a lady
named Julie spoke in tongues during our prayer meeting at
St. Luke's Parish. As soon as she started speaking in tongues,
I was receiving the interpretation in the English language.
The length and emphasis of her delivery was almost the
same length and emphasis of the interpretation that I was
receiving. Thereupon, I started giving the interpretation in
English as soon as she finished speaking in tongues. God is
sovereign, and I'm always in awe of His power and grace!
2. The interpretation could come as an explanation or
commentary of the utterance in tongues.
3. The interpretation could be a paraphrase of the
tongues being spoken. For instance, it may take a person a
minute to deliver God's message in tongues but it may just
take twenty seconds for another person to give the interpretation of the tongues.
I personally have had experiences of giving a much
shorter version of what was being spoken in tongues during
prayer meetings or prayer assemblies.

4. The interpretation could be a gist or a summation of the message given in tongues. Again, when this occurs, chances are that the interpretation of tongues is shorter than what is being spoken in tongues.

I have been asked many times during and after ministering to God's people in many countries throughout the world, about how I proceed in using the gifts of the Holy Spirit.

The leadings, nudgings, revelations, and promptings of the Holy Spirit come to me in myriad ways:

A. Through visions or *mental pictures*. Most of the time, these take place when I'm actually ministering to God's people.

B. Through a still, small voice, speaking directly into my heart, and sometimes I hear an audible voice, directing me to do or say something to individuals or groups of people while I'm ministering in Jesus' name. However, hearing an audible voice from the Lord is a rare occurrence.

C. Through knowledge that I receive in my inner being about what the Lord is doing or directing me to do or say to a certain individual or groups of people who I'm ministering to. In other words, I know and I know, without any iota of a doubt, that this is what the Lord wants me to do or say, and sometimes the Holy Spirit will provide me with the exact words to say.

D. Sometimes, I might feel a *dull pain* on any part of the body that the Lord is healing in that instant or moment for someone else. Usually, this happens during Healing Crusades or Healing Rallies that I have the privilege to conduct.

I would like to summarize my reply to this question:

1. Focus your heart and mind, in fact, your entire being, on the Lord Jesus Christ, who is the leader and perfecter of our faith (Hebrews 12:2).
2. Be hearers and doers of God's words.

Be doers of the word and not hearers only, deluding yourselves. For if anyone is a hearer of the word and not a doer, he is like a man who looks at his own face in a mirror. He sees himself, then goes off and promptly forgets what he looked like. But the one who peers into the perfect law of freedom and perseveres, and is not a hearer who forgets but a doer who acts, such a one shall be blessed in what he does (James 1:22–25).

3. Obey the Lord always! The Word of God says,

"…Obedience is better than sacrifice,
    to listen, better than the fat of rams"
(1 Samuel 15:22).

I fervently believe that if you obey the words of the Lord and His leadings and promptings, you will see things happen far beyond your wildest imagination. For the Lord, nothing is impossible at all.

4. Be humble always before the Lord and before men:

> I, then, a prisoner for the Lord, urge you to live in a manner worthy of the call you have received, with all humility and gentleness, with patience, bearing with one another through love (Ephesians 4:1–2).

In Matthew 23:12, Jesus says, "Whoever exalts himself will be humbled; but whoever humbles himself will be exalted."

The truth is, without the Lord, we are nothing at all. With the Lord on our side, we are victorious in this life and can do anything through Him who strengthens us (see Ephesians chapter 4).

Prayer to Receive the Gift of Interpretation of Tongues

I believe, Lord Jesus,
that nothing is impossible for you.
Endow me with the gift of
interpretation of tongues so that
I will be able to understand and
interpret the message from you that
is being delivered in tongues.
Holy Spirit assist me,
in Jesus' name,
to help my fellow believers
and nonbelievers alike,
to know that you are truly alive and
you are working
among your people
to draw them unto yourself
for your greater glory and honor,
Amen.

Robert calling people by name and giving each person a prophecy and messages from the Holy Spirit through the Spiritual Gifts of Prophecy, Word of Knowledge and Word of Wisdom during the Healing Crusades in Malaysia in 2017.

WORD GIFTS

CHAPTER 13
How to Receive
and Use the Awesome
Power from on High

"Behold, I have given you the
power to 'tread upon serpents'
and scorpions and upon the full
force of the enemy and nothing
will harm you."
—Luke 10:19—

We read in Luke 4:16–21,

> ...He stood up to read and was handed a scroll
> of the prophet Isaiah. He unrolled the scroll
> and found the passage where it was written:

> "The Spirit of the Lord is upon me,
>   because he has anointed me
>   to bring glad tidings to the poor.
> He has sent me to proclaim liberty to captives
>   and recovery of sight to the blind,
>   to let the oppressed go free,
> and to proclaim a year acceptable to the Lord."

> Rolling up the scroll, he handed it back to the attendant and sat down, and the eyes of all in the synagogue looked intently at him. He said to them, "Today this scripture passage is fulfilled in your hearing."

In the Book of John 14:12, Jesus says:

> Amen, amen, I say to you, whoever believes in me will do the works that I do, and will do greater ones than these, because I am going to the Father.

And we read in Acts 1:8:

> But you will receive power when the holy Spirit comes upon you, and you will be my witnesses in Jerusalem, throughout Judea and Samaria, and to the ends of the earth.

From these different passages in the Scriptures, we can say that the Lord's will and design for our lives is to live a power-filled style of living.

The source of this mighty power, this divine power in our lives, is the Holy Spirit. It is not from our own wisdom, knowledge, or ability but from the Holy Spirit and intended to operate in our daily lives.

Many Christians, however, do not live in the power that the Lord wants them to have. They claim for themselves only a minute portion of what God has made possible for them in Christ Jesus because they are ignorant of what the Holy Spirit can do and wants to do for them and through them.

In John 7:37–38, Jesus says:

> On the last and greatest day of the feast, Jesus stood up and exclaimed, "Let anyone who thirsts come to me and drink. Whoever believes in me, as scripture says:
>
> 'Rivers of living water will flow from within him.'"

In Luke 11:13, Jesus says:

> If you then, who are wicked, know how to give good gifts to your children, how much more will the Father in heaven give the holy Spirit to those who ask him?

Some people describe His power as *dunamis*, a Greek word meaning *dynamite*. But I believe that this power that the Lord is giving us is more powerful, more potent than all the atomic bombs and weapons combined in this world. We have an awesome God, and His power is awesome. There is no limit to His power. There is no restriction to His power. His power creates as well as destroys power that is not of Him and from Him. His power is Divine in nature and nothing is more powerful than Divine power.

Allow me to share with you some principles to obtain a power-filled life:

1. Have a constant, moment-by-moment and right personal relationship with Jesus Christ, the Lord.

He should be number one in your life. He should be the King, the Lord, and the Savior of your life 24/7.

> If you remain in me and my words remain in you, ask for whatever you want and it will be done for you. By this is my Father glorified, that you bear much fruit and become my disciples (John 15:7–8).

Every time I read this passage in the Scriptures, a feeling of tremendous excitement starts to *well up* within me.

2. Be an imitator of Christ.

In other words, we should strive to be like Jesus in every way. As a matter of fact, this should be a Christian's number one goal. This goal necessitates for us to talk like Jesus, think like Jesus, act like Jesus, have an attitude like that of Jesus, and do what He commands us to do. Furthermore, it means *dying to self* so that we will be truly *alive in Him* (cf.Romans 6:11).

I believe it is not impossible to achieve this goal. Yes, we can achieve all of these attributes through the power of the Holy Spirit. In Philippians 4:13, St. Paul states: "I have the strength for everything through him who empowers me."

3. Practice constant, day-to-day communications with God.

This is what prayer is—communication with God. We can do it with our eyes closed or opened. We can do it kneeling down or sitting down, or standing up or walking around, or even lying down. We can do it anywhere we are. We can do it with verbal outburst of emotion or without verbal words. Jesus said in Matthew 7:7, "Ask and it will be given to you; seek and you will find; knock and the door will be opened to you."

Now, how many Christians do you think who pray don't really have faith that God is going to do anything great? On the other hand, how many Christians have great faith but don't have the discipline to pray? If we want to see the supernatural take place in our lives, we need to live a lifestyle that is focused on constant communication with God. In Philippians 4:6, St. Paul says, "Have no anxiety at all, but in everything, by prayer and petition, with thanksgiving, make your requests known to God."

In James 4:2–3, we read:

> You covet but do not possess. You kill and envy but you cannot obtain; you fight and wage war. You do not possess because you do not ask. You ask but do not receive, because you ask wrongly, to spend it on your passions.

4. Be filled with the Holy Spirit.

St. Paul says in Ephesians 5:18, "And do not get drunk on wine, in which lies debauchery, but be filled with the Spirit."

Every day, we should ask the Holy Spirit in faith to fill us with His presence, His power, and His grace. In Luke 11:13, Jesus says:

> If you then, who are wicked, know how to give good gifts to your children, how much more will the Father in heaven give the holy Spirit to those who ask him?

5. Obey the Lord's commands and the promptings of His Holy Spirit.

Our obedience to the Lord and His commands for us really moves the heart of God. Only by obedience to the Lord and His commands can we experience the miraculous before our eyes. Remember what the scriptures say in 1 Samuel 15:22.

Testimonial
About Obedience to the Holy Spirit

Hello brother Bob,

Please say my hello to your wife Chita and to your friend, Jim Blubaugh, as well. I am Martina. You prayed over me in 2013, when you conducted a Healing Crusade attended by thousands including Buddhists and Muslims in Kuching Sarawak, Malaysia.

At that time, I was paralyzed. I had been paralyzed for a number of years. You told me to continue to thank and praise Jesus Christ because, "He is healing you for His glory and honor and to let you know and the people here that He is alive and that He is still in the healing business." That was what you told me. Afterwards, you prayed over me and told me to stand up in Jesus' Name. I stood up and walked and walked and I'm still, to this day, walking normally. Jesus fully healed me. Thank you so much. People here are so amazed what happened, and many have been converted to the Roman Catholic religion because they have witnessed many who stood up from their wheelchairs, many blind people able to see again, deaf people no longer using their hearing devices, and many people giving testimonies of healing of cancer and other illnesses. Until now people are still talking about those amazing healings. Truly Jesus is alive and He is still in the healing business as you have proclaimed, and He loves us no matter what.

I'm praying for you and your ministry, and many people here are waiting for you to come back to Malaysia again. I hope you get this testimony this time. I believe when I originally sent this to you, you did not get it for some reason.

Thank you again, brother Bob, for your services to the Lord by being an instrument to heal the sick, and for giving hope to the hopeless.
Sincerely,
Martina Ida Laja Proft
Kuching, Sarawak, Malaysia

6. Saturate your entire being with God's words.

Jesus says, in John 6:63, "It is the spirit that gives life, while the flesh is of no avail. The words I have spoken to you are spirit and life." Psalm 119:105 tells us, "Your word is a lamp for my feet, a light for my path."

Indeed, God's word is power! In Revelation 12:11, the Word of God tells us:

> "They conquered him by the blood
>   of the Lamb
> and by the word of their
>   testimony;…"

The Catechism of the Catholic Church Number 104, states that:

> In Sacred Scripture, the Church constantly finds her nourishment and her strength, for she welcomes it not as a human word, "but as what it really is, the word of God".[1] "In the sacred books, the Father who is in heaven comes lovingly to meet his children, and talks with them."[2]

St. Jerome, one of the Doctors of the Catholic Church, says that "ignorance of Scriptures is ignorance of Christ."

7. Let us avail ourselves of the Sacraments of the Catholic Church, especially the Sacraments of Reconciliation or Confession and the Eucharist.

Catechism of the Catholic Church Number 1422 states:

> "Those who approach the sacrament of Penance obtain pardon from God's mercy for the offense committed against him, and are, at the same time, reconciled with the Church which they have wounded by their sins and which by charity, by example, and by prayer labors for their conversion."[3]

It further maintains,

> Jesus calls to conversion. This call is an essential part of the proclamation of the kingdom: "The time is fulfilled, and the kingdom of God is at hand; repent, and believe in the gospel."[4] In the Church's preaching this call is addressed first to those who do not yet know Christ and his Gospel. Also, Baptism is the principal place for the first and fundamental conversion. It is by faith in the Gospel and by Baptism[5] that one renounces evil and gains salvation, that is, the forgiveness of all sins and the gift of new life (CCC #1427).

In order for God's power or anointing to remain in us, we should also avail ourselves with the Sacrament of the Eucharist daily, if possible. The Holy Eucharist, the Documents of Vatican Council II tells us, is "the source and summit of the Christian life" (Lumen gentium, no. 11; cf. Catechism of the Catholic Church, #1324).

> "At the Last Supper, on the night he was be-
> trayed, our Savior instituted the Eucharistic
> sacrifice of his Body and Blood. This he did
> in order to perpetuate the sacrifice of the
> cross throughout the ages until he should
> come again, and so to entrust to his beloved
> Spouse, the Church, a memorial of his death
> and resurrection: a sacrament of love, a sign
> of unity, a bond of charity, a Paschal banquet
> 'in which Christ is consumed, the mind is
> filled with grace, and a pledge of future glory
> is given to us.'"[6] (CCC # 1323).

We encounter Jesus in a very special way through the Sacraments of the Church. Needless to say, the Sacraments are also great sources of power in a person's life.

Testimonial
About Reconciliation with God

Dear Bro. Bob,

Praise and thanks be to God for His unending love and mercy! Also to Mama Mary for her intercession! A few months ago, I asked you to pray over my cousin Mon from the Philippines who was diagnosed with pancreatic cancer that had metastasized to his liver, and you did pray with him via phone.

He went to confession for the first time in a long time, and he started going to mass and has been receiving the Body and Blood of Jesus and praying the Rosary regularly with his wife, as you advised him to do. My cousin's wife told me that he is a changed person. My cousin has become more closer to our Lord Jesus Christ. Yesterday, I received a message from his wife that his PET SCAN results came back showing that the lesions in his liver had disappeared and the tumor in his pancreas has shrunk significantly!

Thank you Bob for your prayers. I believe my cousin received his miraculous healings not only physically but also spiritually, which is very important. Please continue to pray for his complete healing—physically, mentally, and spiritually. God is truly good and merciful.

To God be the glory! May God bless you and your family abundantly for all that you do.

Love,

Fe Lacbain

Oxnard, California

8. Have an expectant faith, a kind of faith that can move mountains.

What is the Biblical definition of faith? Faith is the realization of what is hoped for and evidence of things not seen (Hebrews11:1).

In Luke 17:6, Jesus says:

> The Lord replied, "If you have faith the size of a mustard seed, you would say to [this] mulberry tree, 'Be uprooted and planted in the sea,' and it would obey you.

But without faith it is impossible to please him,... (Hebrews 11:6).

Faith is one of the gifts of the Holy Spirit. It is God's will for us to have a supernatural kind of faith, a faith that can move mountains.

We are all unworthy to be used by the Lord. Early on in my preaching, teaching, and healing ministry, I reminded the Lord that I am unworthy and I feel unworthy to be a vessel of His power. He spoke into my heart. He said, "My son, I shed my precious blood for you on the Cross at Calvary. By doing so, I made you worthy of my love for you." I, then, asked Him to grant me the faith that can move mountains.

Faith can move the heart of God.

How to Use God's Awesome Power

Following are six guidelines with scriptures to help you build your faith and learn how to use God's awesome power.

1. Use it in the Name of Jesus and by the power of His Holy Spirit.

In Philippians 2:9–11, St. Paul says:

Because of this, God greatly exalted him
    and bestowed on him the name
    that is above every name,
    that at the name of Jesus
    every knee should bend,
    of those in heaven and on earth and under the earth,
    and every tongue confess that
    Jesus Christ is Lord,
    to the glory of God the Father.

In November 2007, a lady called from Michigan asking me to pray with her over the telephone for the dead fetus in her womb. She said,

> I'm four months pregnant, but tomorrow the doctors will have to remove the dead fetus from my womb. I am very scared of the doctor's procedures and very distraught over what happened to my baby.

She said all the tests had confirmed the demise of the baby in her womb. As we started to pray, I sensed that the Lord wanted me to speak life into the dead fetus. So, I followed the promptings of the Holy Spirit. I spoke life into the baby at least three times in the mighty Name of Jesus. But I didn't hear from the lady again until February 2008, which was three months later.

When I spoke with the lady, she told me that she just delivered a healthy, eight-pound baby girl. When I asked her what happened, she said that the day the doctors were to remove the "dead" fetus, they had detected heartbeats instead during the ultrasound and other tests.

Truly, there is power in the Name of Jesus if we invoke it with love and reverence, and with expectant faith.

2. Use it for God's glory.

In 1 Corinthians 10:31, St. Paul says, "So whether you eat or drink, or whatever you do, do everything for the glory of God." All honor and glory rightfully belong to God alone, for, without Him, we are nothing and we cannot do anything (cf. John 15:5).

When I pray for the sick for instance, I always ask the Lord for His Name to be glorified through the healing of the person.

Testimonial
to the Glory to God

Approximately more than two years ago, in August of 2016, I was diagnosed with Ovarian cancer/peritoneal carcinomatosis, stage 3. My surgeon told me that he was unable to operate on me due to the size of my ovaries, which were as big as an orange, and a growth in my peritoneal cavity as large as a dinner plate. So, he recommended for me to undergo chemotherapy once a week for four months before surgery, then for two more months after surgery.

Two weeks before the surgery was to be performed, I attended the Mass and Healing Service at St. Luke's Parish gym in Stockton, California. Bob Canton, who was conducting the Healing Service, called out healings of people who were having problems in their stomach areas, GI, abdomen, and internal organs. He asked for those people to come forward in front of the gym to be prayed over for complete healing.

When Bob touched my forehead, I went down on the floor. As he was praying over me while I was lying down on the floor, I felt heat radiating from my head down to my stomach area. Bob told me not to be afraid because "the Lord is with you, and Jesus will not forsake nor leave you." I also heard Bob saying, "Lord, heal her for your greater glory and honor."

Two weeks later, a surgery was performed.

The surgery room was reserved for four to six hours in anticipation for other procedures that might be necessary. Nervous and scared, I asked the Lord and Blessed Mother to hold me and stay with me in the operating room. As I was wheeled to the operating room, the last words I heard from my sisters were, "God bless you doctor, please take care of her." The surgery only took two hours.

No other complications or extra procedures were necessary. When the surgeon visited me in the recovery room, he said "the surgery went well." I jokingly asked him if I could have a little souvenir of what he removed from my ovary. He said "no, everything will be sent to the laboratory for further study." When I finally got a copy of the Pathology reports, we were all amazed that there was no cancer nor any tumors that could be found in the ovaries. There was a small note that stated, "there seemed to be a tumor there at one time but no trace of it was found nor detected.

"Praise the Lord." The CA 125 diagnostic marker when I was diagnosed back in July of 2016, was 1877. The normal range is only 30. The marker value went down to 30, then to 7, and now to 3.

To this day, it is still at 3, which is almost nothing, praise the Lord.

My two sisters, Christine, with heart problems, and Joy, with ear and hearing problems, came to attend the prayer meeting at St. Luke's while they were visiting from Las Vegas one Saturday in 2017. They also received healing prayers from the prayer group members.

My sister, Christine's, heart is now functioning like a heart of a teenager according to the doctor and my sister, Joy's, hearing is very much improved after she received prayers. Thank you Jesus, thank you Blessed Mother, thank you Bro. Bob Canton, and all the members of the Children of God Prayer Community of St. Luke's for having a very welcoming attitude and for helping many people like my sisters and me.

What Bro. Bob Canton said during one of the prayer meetings we attended, I repeat here: "God is good, all the time."

Liz Pahati-Tupas,
Stockton, California

3. Use it with humility.

There is nothing that can block, warp, or dilute the power of God except pride.

Psalm 18:28 says, "For humble people you save; / haughty eyes you bring low." Therefore, the more humble we become, the more power and anointing from God will reside upon us.

1 Peter 5:5 reads:

> Likewise, you younger members, be subject to the presbyters. And all of you, clothe yourselves with humility in your dealings with one another, for:

> "God opposes the proud
>   but bestows favor on the humble."

Jesus Himself is the model of humility par excellence. According to St. Paul in Philippians 2:5–8:

> Have among yourselves the same attitude
> that is also yours in Christ Jesus,

> Who, though he was in the form
>   of God,
>   did not regard equality with God
>   something to be grasped.
>   Rather, he emptied himself,
>   taking the form of a slave,
>   coming in human likeness;
>   and found human in
>   appearance,
>   he humbled himself,
>   becoming obedient to death,
>   even death on a cross.

4. Use it with boldness.

We should always remember that "the Kingdom of God is not only a matter of words but of power." (cf. 1Corinthians 4:20).

The power of God should be used with boldness in the Holy Spirit. When the power of God is unleashed in our midst to further the Kingdom of God, it will always accomplish its intended purposes. In 2 Timothy 1:7, St. Paul wrote, "For God did not give us a spirit of cowardice but rather of power and love and self-control."

In Acts 4:31, the word of God says:

> As they prayed, the place where they were gathered shook, and they were all filled with the holy Spirit and continued to speak the word of God with boldness.

My brothers and sisters, because of their boldness in the Holy Spirit, the apostles and the disciples had turned this world upside down and inside out, and this world has never been the same since. And the good news is that we are also called by the Lord to do the same by virtue of our baptism.

5. Use it in love.

Love is the key that opens the Kingdom and the heart of God.

In 1 Cor. 13:13, the word of God says, "So faith, hope, love remain, these three; but the greatest of these is love."

For sure, if we use God's power with love, everything will be possible for us. 1 John 4:16 reads:

> We have come to know and to believe in the love God has for us.

God is love, and whoever remains in love remains in God and God in him.

6. Use the gift to build up others.

And he gave some as apostles, others as
prophets, others as evangelists, others as pas-
tors and teachers, to equip the holy ones for
the work of ministry, for building up the body
of Christ, until we all attain to the unity of
faith and knowledge of the Son of God, to
mature manhood, to the extent of the full
stature of Christ,.... (Ephesians 4:11–13)

Chapter 13 Endnotes

1. 1 Thes 2:13; cf. DV 24.
2. DV 21.
3. LG 11 # 2.
4. Mk 1:15.
5. Cf. Acts 2:38.
6. SC 47.

Healing and Keeping Prayer

"Heavenly Father, I thank you for loving me. I thank you for sending your Son, Our Lord Jesus Christ, to the world to save and to set me free. I trust in your power and grace that sustain and restore me. Loving Father, touch me now with your healing hands, for I believe that your will is for me to be well in my mind, body, soul, and spirit. Cover me with the most precious blood of your Son, our Lord Jesus Christ, from the top of my head to the soles of my feet. Cast out anything that should not be in me. Root out any unhealthy and abnormal cells and all causes of sickness from my entire body. Open any blocked arteries or veins and rebuild and replenish any damaged areas. Remove all inflammation and cleanse any infection by the power of Jesus' precious Blood. Let the fire of your healing love pass through my entire body to heal and make new any diseased areas so that my body will function the way you created it to function. Fortify all my organs, all the systems in my body, all my arteries, blood vessels and veins, all my healthy tissues and cells, all my bones, joints, and ligaments, and all my nerves and muscles in my body by the power of your Holy Spirit. Touch also my mind and my emotion, even the deepest recesses of my heart. Saturate my entire being with your presence, love, joy, and peace and draw me ever closer to you every moment of my life. And Father, fill me with your Holy Spirit and empower me to do your works so that my life will bring glory and honor to your holy name. I ask this in the name of the Lord Jesus Christ, Amen."

Prayer for Empowerment

"Lord Jesus Christ, thank you for
loving me, thank you for dying for
me on the cross. Because of your
death and resurrection you have
redeemed and set me free. Have
mercy on me, forgive me of all my
sins. I surrender myself to you.
I surrender to you my heart, my
mind, my soul and my spirit, my
will, my entire body and my entire being. I am totally yours and I
give you permission to do unto me
as you will. I invite you to come
into my life and be the Lord and
King and Savior and Deliverer
and Healer of my life. I renounce
Satan and all his empty works, and
all his empty promises. Cover me
Lord Jesus with your most precious
Blood from the top of my head to
the soles of my feet, and protect
me from the attacks and traps and
tactics of the evil one. Send your
Holy Spirit to strengthen and to
empower me, to guide and to help
me become more like you in every
way. Come Holy Spirit and pour
out on me your gifts and your fruit

so that my life will give glory to the
Holy Trinity. Mary, Mother Most
Holy, and Mother of my Savior,
Mother of God, Mother of the
Messiah, pray for me throughout
all the days of my life. Let the
mantle of your love and healing
and protection be upon me always.
I also ask all the ministering angels
in heaven, the angels of powers
and virtues, the angels of healings
and miracles, the angels of love
and peace and joy, the angels of
safety and protection, the angels of
victory, Saints Michael, Gabriel,
and Raphael and the archangels
and legions of angels in heaven, to
encamp around me and minister to
me and to all my loved ones all the
days of our lives. I ask all of these,
in the mighty and powerful Name
of Jesus, my Lord, Amen."

Spiritual Warfare Prayer

"Lord Jesus, you are my Savior and my deliverer. I thank you for dying for me on the Cross, because through your death and resurrection, you have set me free. I renounce right now any and all allegiance that I have ever given to Satan and his host of evil spirits. I resist them and I refuse to be intimidated or be used by them in any way whatsoever. I rebuke all their attacks upon my body, my emotion, my mind and spirit in the mighty name and by the power of the shed Blood of the Lord Jesus Christ and through the mantle of Mary, the Immaculate Conception.
In Jesus' name, I break the transmission of any and all satanic vows, spiritual bonds, pacts, soul ties, and demonic works. I dissolve any and all curses, hexes, spells, traps, snares, obstacles, deceptions, lies, evil desires, evil wishes, hereditary seals, and every disease, infirmity, and affliction from any source including my mistakes and sins by the Blood of Jesus.

In Jesus' Name, I break and dissolve any and all evil effects or ties associated with astrologers, clairvoyants, channelers, charters, crystals and crystal healers, mediums, fortune tellers, occult seers, palm, tea leaf, or tarot card readers, psychics, satanic cults, santeros, quack doctors, spirit guides, witches, witch-doctors, superstitious beliefs and practices, and the new age movement. By the precious Blood of Jesus, I break and dissolve all effects of participation in seances and divination, Ouija boards, horoscopes, occult games, and any form of worship that does not offer true honor and recognition of the Holy Trinity and the Lordship of Jesus Christ. I stand secure upon the promises in the power of the Cross of Calvary whereby Satan and all his cohorts became defeated foes through the shed blood of the Lord Jesus Christ. I stand upon and claim all the promises of God's Word. In humble faith, I do here and now put on the whole armor of God that protects and enables me to do battle and to stand firm against the schemes and tactics of the evil one.

In faith, I cover myself, my loved

ones, and all of our possessions with the precious Blood of Jesus Christ. Lord Jesus, I give you praise and honor and glory. You are the Victor over all evil and all glory belongs to you. Fill me now with your Holy Spirit and help me to become more like you. Mary, Help of Christians, I entreat you to place your mantle of protection upon me for you have crushed the head of the ancient serpent.

I also ask for the protection of the angels in heaven, the angels of powers and virtues and healings, the angels of love and joy and peace, the angels of safety and protection, Saints Michael, Gabriel, and Raphael and all the legions of angels to surround me and to minister to me and my loved ones all the days of our lives. I ask this in Jesus' Name and through the power of the Holy Spirit, Amen."

A Personal Note from Robert Canton

I encourage everyone to pray the "Healing and Keeping Prayer" every day, including the prayer for healing for a specific type of sickness or disease. I would also like to recommend everyone to pray the "Prayer for Empowerment" and the "Spiritual Warfare Prayer" daily.

You may download a copy of these prayers by accessing my website at www.RobertCantonMinistries.org and distribute them to your friends and loved ones or to the sick. If you have some testimonies after reading this book, please send them to rccanton@sbcglobal.net for the greater glory and honor of God. God bless you!

Robert speaking at a Healing Crusade in Singapore.